DID NOT BELIEVE

Misadventures in Running, Cycling and Swimming
(Book Seven in the DNF Series)

This edition published 2022 by George Mahood.

www.facebook.com/georgemahood
www.instagram.com/georgemahood
www.twitter.com/georgemahood
www.georgemahood.com

ONE

After the turmoil of 2020, there was hope for a return to normality in 2021. Then Covid cases rose rapidly, Christmas was cancelled, and the UK entered its third lockdown in January 2021.

The government insisted it would not close schools like it had during the first lockdown. After the Christmas holiday, children returned to school.

For one day.

Just to give them all a chance to spread a little Covid around between classmates. And then the government decided it would close schools after all.

At the time of the first lockdown in March 2020, my wife Rachel had been working as a supply teacher and all her work disappeared when schools closed. From September 2020, when children returned to schools, Rachel began a contracted teaching job at the local primary school working four days a week. When schools closed again in January 2021, her job continued. Rachel's role was to remotely teach children who needed additional help with their work during lockdown.

That left me in charge of homeschooling our three children: Kitty aged 9, Leo aged 11 and Layla aged 13.

Children of keyworkers were allowed to go to school as normal, and they were taught in small bubbles in their classrooms. As a teacher, Rachel classified as a keyworker, so we could have sent our children into school. But I'm not a keyworker. The functioning of society does not depend upon my books. I could not justify sending them into school during a pandemic while I wrote stupid stories on my computer. Sending the children into school simply because Rachel was a keyworker, while I sat at home and pretended to work, would be taking the piss. With the alternative prospect of homeschooling, I think Rachel quite enjoyed escaping to an empty classroom each day to teach children remotely.

I knew I was unlikely to get any writing done while homeschooling three children, but I don't have to work during the school day. I could, if I chose, do my work in the evenings, or even after the children have gone to bed. I rarely do choose this, but that's my own fault. So Layla, Leo and Kitty remained at home throughout lockdown and we got by as best we could.

The schools were more prepared this time and homeschooling was very different to during the first lockdown. Layla is at secondary school and all her lessons happened remotely as if she was at school. She sat at her computer for the entire school day, and the teachers taught the classes remotely.

Leo and Kitty had daily class video calls with their class teacher, but the majority of their work was sent over first thing each morning and they could complete it in their own time during the day.

Most of their assignments came through to us via video links. Our Wi-Fi is so slow that it took the best part of an hour to even watch the 10-minute instructional video about the day's tasks.

We can, however, get 4G at the top of a big hill about half a mile from our house. So each morning, once the notification had arrived to let me know the day's work was available, our dog Ludo and I walked up the hill and I downloaded all the relevant videos onto my phone. At various points during the day, additional videos were added, so Ludo and I had to make the trip multiple times. By the end of day three I had already exceeded my phone's data allowance, so had to upgrade to a new contract.

PE with Joe returned. Fitness instructor Joe Wicks resumed his live YouTube morning workouts again - this time just Monday, Wednesday and Friday. I tried to persuade the children to join me, but I was on my own from the start.

January and February were cold and wet and by the time the school day ended it was already dark outside. It was a far bleaker experience that the stunning spring weather we had during the first lockdown.

I did my January 10k a day challenge for the third year. This year it took on more of a significance after a day homeschooling. In previous years, it had often felt a chore to fit in the run. This time I looked forward to it. Many of my runs were in the dark, or the rain, or often both, but it still felt amazing to be free for a while. Occasionally, to take a break from homeschooling, Layla, Leo and Kitty joined me on their bikes during the day while I ran. Most of those ended in an argument. Usually between Kitty and her bike.

Homeschooling three children was pretty full on. I kept having to remind myself that in years to come I would hopefully look back fondly with rose-tinted glasses at this time. It was a unique situation and one that was unlikely to happen ever again while our children were at school. So I tried to embrace it.

It wasn't all bad. Some of their work assignments were fun. As part of their science and forest school lessons, we had to go on walks and look for certain things in the local countryside. For art, they had to make an artistic mosaic from leaves and other items found in nature. Kitty once had to build a giant bird's nest out of sticks (I'm not sure what the purpose of this was, but it was quite enjoyable).

For science Leo had to build bridges out of newspaper and calculate how much weight they could support. When the experiment was over, Rachel put the bridge in the recycling bin. The following week, Leo's assignment was to try some new bridge-building techniques to improve the original structure. So we fished it out of the recycling bin, patched it up, made some improvements, and redid the experiment. The following week we needed it again, so had to retrieve it from the bin once more, where Rachel had tidied it away. Needless to say, it did not look structurally sound by the end.

Towards the end of term, Ofsted school inspectors assessed the primary school's homeschooling. As if things weren't challenging enough for the staff having to adapt to teaching during a global pandemic, they then got to have their practises scrutinised by a team of assessors too. As part of their report, the inspectors asked to see more feedback given to the work children were submitting via the online learning platform. Teachers were also encouraged to get children to take their work on to the next level. I found persuading the children to do the work in the first place was a fair old slog, and now we had to deal with the Ofsted required follow-ups too. I would usually get all of their work uploaded by about 4pm, only to check my phone an hour later to see lots of additional questions about the work.

Leo's class studied the peppered moth for a couple of weeks. The peppered moth is a white moth, with black speckles on its wings. It is an example of natural selection and its wing colour and pattern evolved during times of high levels of air pollution during the industrial revolution. As part of his art, Leo was required to draw a peppered moth.

Leo is quite creative, but his drawing skills are a little...
er... (how do I put this politely?) basic. All three children
make Rachel and me birthday cards each year. Layla's and
Kitty's are always bright and colourful, and they spend
quite a lot of time and effort on them. Leo's are always
drawn in pencil, there is never any colour, he favours the
minimalist approach, and rarely devotes more than about
30 seconds to the card marking.

I encouraged him to devote a little more time to his
peppered moth, and he produced - by his standards - quite
a good drawing. We submitted it to the teacher. The
feedback came in later that day.

*I can see what meaning you were trying to portray, but it doesn't
have the atmosphere I'd expect to go with this meaning. Maybe you
could put this in front of an industrial background? Also, would your
moth have a smiley face?*

She had a point.

The photo was definitely lacking atmosphere. But it had
taken Leo a fair amount of time to draw, and it was now
the end of the day and I was fucking bored with peppered
moths. However, the teacher needed Leo to respond to the
feedback. Ofsted insisted on it. So we responded.

The teacher was also right about the smile. The moth
should not have had a smiley face. First, I'm not sure moths
do smile. Second, it lived through a time of high air
pollution so had little to smile about. Leo rubbed out the
smiley face and drew a screaming face instead.

Maybe you could put this in front of an industrial background?

That was a good idea from the teacher, too. Why didn't we think of that? So we lay his artwork on a pile of coal and took another photo. It was an improvement, but we still felt it was lacking in atmosphere.

So we set fire to it.

We played out the dramatic *O Fortuna* by Carl Orff in the background and filmed the drawing of the moth as it burned, its screaming face visible throughout.

And then Leo submitted the video in response to the teacher's feedback and included the comment:

I have tried to make my artwork a bit more dramatic.

As he clicked *submit* I became a little nervous about whether we had overstepped the mark.

Rachel returned from school an hour later.

'I hear you've been having fun at homeschool today?' she said.

'Oh no. What have you heard?'

'Leo's year six teacher paid me a visit this afternoon. She showed me the video.'

'Uh oh. And?'

'And then she went and showed it to the head teacher.'

'Oh god.'

Leo looked a bit mortified. Rachel pulled a stern face and gave a long dramatic pause.

'They all thought it was hilarious,' she said. 'It really made us all laugh. Leo, I can't believe you burnt your artwork!'

'I was creating an even better artwork. More atmospheric.'

'It certainly was atmospheric.'

'Can I burn my school work now and film it?' said Layla.

'Don't you dare!' said Rachel.

It became increasingly difficult to keep everyone's motivation up. Towards the end of term, Kitty's enthusiasm for homeschooling began to flag too (mine disappeared in the second week of January). Kitty's science assignments were a particular bugbear, and during one activity on photosynthesis, she laid her head on her schoolwork on the table and stayed like that for ten minutes. Rather than continue with the science assignment, I took a photo of her with her head on the table and submitted that as her day's work, with the comment:

This is as far as we got with today's science. Sorry.

TWO

During the previous summer, I went for a bike ride with my friend Simon early one morning. We passed a motorbike parked at a bridge with a cameraman seated on the back.

'What are you filming?' asked Simon.

'The Royal Marines Iron Challenge,' the cameraman said. 'The cyclists will be through here any minute now.'

'What is the Royal Marines Iron Challenge?' I asked. 'I've never heard of it.'

'No, it's a brand new event. This is just a sort of tester year. It's a full iron-distance triathlon. 2.4 mile sea swim, 112 mile bike ride and then a full coastal path marathon.'

'Is it likely to happen again next year?'

'That's the plan. They want to open it up to the public.'

'Huh.'

And with that *huh*, a seed had been sown.

Then another two lockdowns happened and I forgot all about the Royal Marines Iron Challenge and sort of assumed that no events would ever happen again.

I didn't think about the Royal Marines Iron Challenge again until March 2021, just as we were coming out of the third lockdown. Sophie, a friend of ours, had signed up out of the blue. A couple of other friends were also tempted. It was actually happening.

The event would take place in the middle of September, later that year. I had been reluctant to do another iron-distance triathlon, as I wanted to avoid getting obsessed about training or trying to beat my previous time. This one made all of those concerns irrelevant. The course was so challenging that getting personal bests was not a consideration. Crossing the finish line would be the only goal.

The organisers had done some calculations and concluded that the Royal Marines Iron Challenge was probably in the top four toughest iron-distance triathlons in the world. The fact that it was taking place so close to where we live made it seem like too good of an opportunity to turn down. There was one thing that would seal the deal.

I wanted Rachel to do it, too.

I mentioned it to her and she laughed at me in the same way she had when I first suggested she try running, then signing up for a half-marathon, marathon, triathlon, half-ironman and an ultramarathon. She did not believe she was capable.

'Ha, very funny. There is NO way I am doing an ironman.'

'You said that about every other challenge you have taken on.'

'Those were different. An ironman is an ironman.'

'There is no difference. It's just the next stage. It's just more of the same.'

'I'm not doing it. Not a chance.'

'Sophie has signed up. And I think Claire is considering it as well.'

'Sophie has signed up? And Claire is going too? Really?' Rachel's entire manner changed completely.

Later that evening, we both signed up.

THREE

Rachel and I were still doing our marathon-a-month challenge which began in January 2020. I had been reluctant to continue it into 2021, but after Rachel knocked out a January marathon, I knew it was inevitable I would follow suit. In January I ran with my friend Tim. We deliberately chose a route avoiding too many hills and completed my first ever sub-4-hour self-supported marathon. In February I did a much slower coastal loop on my own.

Schools reopened in March and for Rachel's 42nd birthday, she decided to run 42 miles. Unable to think of a suitable route, I suggested a local loop of the town we often run that happens to be 4.2 miles.

'You could just do that ten times. That's 42 miles,' I said.

'Yeah right. That would be so boring.'

'It might be a bit, but it's a nice varied loop and if you're doing loops, you could leave all your food and drink somewhere rather than carry it.'

'Hmmmm.'

So the following day, she ran ten loops. She asked me to join her, but someone had to take the kids to school and walk the dog. Plus, I was still only 41.

I joined her for a 'few' loops in between school runs, and managed just under 30 miles, which more than satisfied my March marathon. It was surprisingly enjoyable running loops. The lap was long and varied enough that it didn't feel like we were running around in circles, and there was something reassuring about the familiarity of it all. Some friends of Rachel's joined her for a couple of laps, and we got some odd looks from builders who saw us pass them regularly.

With lockdown restrictions due to be lifted in April, and an increasing desire for us to go away somewhere for a few days, I booked four nights in a caravan in a holiday park on the Lizard Peninsula in Cornwall during the Easter holidays.

As soon as we crossed the Tamar bridge into Cornwall, the traffic was backed up along the A38, with thousands of families all doing the same. I did momentarily regret booking a holiday for the day lockdown restrictions eased.

But as we turned off onto the more remote part of the Lizard peninsula, the vast majority of vehicles continued on towards the more popular holiday destinations of St Ives, Padstow and Newquay.

Rachel had completed her April marathon early in the month, and we arrived in Cornwall on April the 12th. We were signed up to an extremely tough event on May the 1st so I didn't want to leave my marathon much later in the month. I also didn't really want to do it during our holiday in Cornwall, as it would be disruptive.

'Why don't you do it now?' said Rachel, as we parked the van outside our caravan.

'Now? As in this evening?'

'Yes, it's 2.30. It won't be dark until about 8ish, so you've got plenty of time.'

'Hmmm,' I said, not excited at all about the thought of running a marathon and thinking instead of having a beer in the sun on the decking. 'No, I don't think so.'

I unloaded all the bikes from the bike rack and helped bring all the bags into the caravan. Then the marathon idea started to warm to me. It would get it over and done with. And a beer on the decking would taste even better after a long run.

'Are you sure you don't mind?' I said.

'Of course not. The van is all unloaded, and the kids can put their own stuff away. We can get a takeaway when you're back. If you hurry up.'

So I put on a pair of trainers and headed out for a run.

I had done a few spontaneous marathons in the past. But heading off within ten minutes of a four hour car journey was a new level of spontaneity for me. It is not something I would recommend. I had seized up after being behind the wheel for so long and began my marathon still folded in half.

It was the first time in a long while that I had got to explore an area of coastline I hadn't visited before. And the Lizard more than lived up to the hype.

The lizard is the most southerly point of the British mainland. It gets its name from the old Cornish word for fortress - *Lis-ardh*. I headed west and ran through the fishing village of Cadgwith Cove that felt like something from an Enid Blyton novel. A group of four fishermen sat in the sun on the wall below the boathouse, each with a pint in hand. Onward I ran to Devil's Frying Pan, which is an impressive rock arch formed after the collapse of a sea cave in 1868. In rough weather, the sea appears to boil, which gave the place its name. On the day I passed, it hadn't even reached a gentle simmer.

It was a beautiful evening to be out and I had slowly loosened up after the long car journey. Living close to the sea in South Devon, I am used to spectacular coastline, but every headland I rounded on the Lizard made me gasp. And despite the busyness of the roads coming into Cornwall, the South West Coast Path was deserted.

I passed the RNLI lifeboat station above Kilcobben Cove. It sits towards the base of a steep cliff, accessed via some steep steps or a winched cage, and the log flume-style slipway into the sea must result in some dramatic launches, particularly during rough seas. I continued on around the stunning Housel Bay, with the turquoise waters below and the Housel Bay Hotel sitting right on the coast path. I made a mental note to come and visit again one day.

Between leaving the campsite and reaching Lizard point, I passed two other people in about six miles. Lizard Point itself was quite busy with people posing for photos at mainland Britain's most southerly point. When I say 'quite busy', there were six others. Our fears of Cornwall being rammed were unfounded. I too stopped for a photo. With 60 million people on the island, it did feel quite cool to be the most southerly of the lot. If only for ten seconds.

I had been told that the Lizard peninsula is fairly flat. They lied. The inland areas of the peninsula are relatively flat as there are no river estuaries carving up the landscape. But the coastline is anything but. The coast path climbs up and down constantly into various coves, each more stunning than the one before.

Kynance Cove is one of the most photographed beaches in Britain. I had seen many pictures on social media over the years, with its tropical waters and stunning rock formations. I had assumed these photos were heavily filtered or taken on rare sunny days in August. But it looks every bit as good as it does in the photos. And it, too, was empty. It was after 5pm now, but I felt extremely lucky to have the entire beach to myself. The tide was low, so I was able to take the shorter route across the boulder-strewn beach, where I marvelled at the views from the other side before turning to retrace my steps back towards the campsite.

I was still a long way off halfway, but I thought I would explore a bit of the coastline beyond the campsite to the east. And then, if I did run out of light, I would at least be closer to home.

Running back past the campsite was a bad idea. It required a lot of mental discipline to resist the temptation to stop. I could just end my run and go and have a beer as the sun went down. But I knew then that these 15 miles would effectively be wasted. If I wanted to keep up the marathon-a-month challenge, I would have to go out some other day in the next two weeks.

I had to get it done now, so I begrudgingly headed on. Kennack Sands was a short stroll from our campsite and was the nicest swim spot I had seen since Kynance Cove. It got me excited about regular swims during our little holiday.

From Kennack Sands, the coast path climbed again with blackened areas of gorse to either side. A month earlier, strong winds and a prolonged dry spell had caused a series of fires along this stretch of coast. An hour or so earlier, I had been gazing in wonder at the turquoise waters of one of the most beautiful bays I had ever seen. Now it felt like I was in some post-apocalyptic dystopia.

My mood was tumbling too. The distance on my watch hardly moved as I trudged up each of the relentless hills. Downas Cove and the one after that (I've blanked its name from my memory) broke me. I was 18 miles into my run, which for me is always the worst part. Once I am beyond 20 miles, I usually feel better psychologically as 6.2 miles (10km) seems quite achievable. Even if it is a 6.2 mile hobble. 8 miles, however, seems a far more daunting task, especially when the steepness of the valleys causes your speed to plummet to less than 2mph.

I had hoped to continue all the way to the town of Coverack and then retrace my steps along the coast path to get back to the campsite before dark. But not only did the severity of these hills mean I would not be back before dark, mentally I couldn't face the thought of tackling those steep-sided gorges again on the return journey. I was well and truly defeated.

All was not lost, however. I could perhaps still continue my marathon on easier footpaths away from the coast. Or maybe, dare I say it, on some tarmac.

I pulled out my phone and opened the Ordnance Survey app. Halfway up the next hill, there was a footpath off to the left that would lead me onto a network of minor roads and bridleways back in the direction of the campsite. And they looked very flat on the map. But then so did the coast path, providing you didn't pay any attention to the contour lines.

It felt like a relief to at least be heading back towards the campsite without the prospect of more valleys to navigate. I reached a farm gateway and the OS app showed it was a public footpath. There was no footpath sign, but I was dependant on this shortcut, so continued through the gate where the footpath should have been. Five minutes later, a herd of lively bullocks ran at me, clearly not used to having visitors. I stood my ground and they thankfully stopped short a couple of metres from me. I wasn't so interesting to them when not running, so I walked slowly to the stile at the end of the field and continued on my way.

Rachel had ordered burgers from the campsite restaurant. It was already 7.30pm and I still had three miles to go. I couldn't face passing the campsite yet again, so turned into the campsite and ran up to our caravan.

'Yey! You made it!' said Rachel. 'I'm just about to go and collect our food.'

'No, I've still got nearly three miles to go. I'm just going to do laps of the campsite.'

'Ha, ok. Well, you'll be done soon. Well done!'

I completed the distance with about 10 laps of the campsite. Passing our caravan every few minutes and catching a whiff of the burger and chips gave me an incentive to keep going. I finished in the dark just after 8pm, 5 hours and 23 minutes after I started. My burger and chips were still warm, and I demolished the lot before the children had finished theirs.

With lockdown restrictions only just lifted, I expected a bit of hostility from Cornish locals as thousands of us tourists descended on them. Our heavily loaded van, with four bikes mounted on the back and a paddleboard strapped to the roof, meant we weren't exactly travelling incognito. I half expected tyres to be slashed, and signs telling us to go home. From the moment we passed into Cornwall, however, we met nothing but kind and welcoming people. Particularly those in the campsite, and the cafes and shops we visited. It had been an incredibly tough time for everyone for the past year, and many businesses had not survived. Those that were still going were delighted to have us tourists back.

As the vaccination roll-out in the UK continued, I noticed a definite change in attitude amongst the older generation. During the pandemic, I had always made a point of giving a wide berth to anyone I passed when out walking or running. But even if I was on the opposite side of the road, many people I passed would almost dive into the hedge at the sight of me approaching.

Now vaccinated (and some already having their second dose), many of these previously vulnerable people felt invincible. I was the one to sometimes have to back away as an elderly person invaded my personal space for an intimate conversation.

During our holiday in Cornwall, I asked an elderly lady for directions while we were out in the van. She was walking along the pavement on the opposite side of the road, but she abandoned her shopping trolley and skipped across the road to where we were parked.

'Yes, my dear. You need to follow the road all the way to the top of town...'

She then proceeded to lean into the van so far that her face was almost inches from mine. I was forced to lean back so far that I almost joined Rachel in the passenger seat.

'Oh, you don't need to worry about me,' she said, sensing my fear. 'I'm double jabbed!'

I loved seeing this switch in confidence. For a year, people had lived in deep fear of being too close to other people. It was wonderful to see that many of the vulnerable no longer felt so vulnerable, and the control that Covid had over our lives was beginning to weaken.

FOUR

Britain has several recognised coast to coast routes for walking, running and cycling. I had read an article about the Cornish Coast to Coast and thought it would be a fun activity to do with the kids while on holiday in Cornwall. Following the route of the old mineral tramway, the Cornish Coast to Coast is an off-road multi-use trail between the town of Portreath on the north coast, and the village of Devoran on the south.

As it follows the route of old railroads, it has a relatively easy gradient. But the primary appeal, from my point of view as the parent of reluctant cyclists, is that the entire route is just 11 miles.

I thought cycling there and back might be a bit ambitious to do with the children. Also, Ludo would be fine running 11 miles, but even he would struggle with twice the distance.

Ludo is great at running alongside bikes when he's off the lead, but it would be dangerous and risky for us to take him on a busy trail with him on a lead while we cycled. We tried to hire a dog trailer, but they were all fully booked. Rachel decided she would run the entire thing with Ludo, and I would cycle with the three children.

'But won't we be much too quick for you?' I said.

'Have you forgotten what it's like cycling with children?' she said. 'I think me and Ludo will be much too quick for you.'

'Hmm, we'll see about that.'

Psychologically, it seemed easier to cycle the trail north to south. When I showed the children the route on the map, to them (and Rachel and me) it looked downhill all the way.

We all drove to the north end of the trail at Portreath, where I dropped Rachel, the children, Ludo and four bikes off. They played on the beach and had an ice cream, while I drove to Devoran at the southern end of the trail and cycled the 11 miles back to Portreath. That way, we would have the van waiting for us at the end.

It was a fantastic route with a nice easy gradient, gently climbing to the midway point and then gradually descending for the second half. The trail had a gravel surface and was very bumpy and rocky in places. I was riding my road bike, which meant for quite an uncomfortable trip, but that was my fault, not the trail's.

I made it to Portreath in about an hour and found the others at a small play area by the start of the trail. Kitty had a face like thunder before we set off. Leo had done something to annoy her on the swings, and she was determined to have a crap time.

Kitty has a longstanding hate/hate relationship with cycling. There have been occasional moments of enjoyment over the years, but for the most part, she is adamant that bikes are evil.

From the start, the four of us on bikes shot off ahead, leaving Rachel and Ludo in our dust. We had travelled less than 200 metres before one of them needed to stop for a drink break. By which point, Rachel and Ludo caught us and disappeared ahead. We regained the lead but Kitty had to stop because her socks were annoying her. For the first couple of miles, I did my best to stay positive and encourage Kitty. My efforts were futile and my patience was tested to the limits. There was the occasional short stretch that was bumpy and challenging to cycle along, where I did have some sympathy for Kitty, but the rest of it was a joy. My sympathy disappeared completely when I heard her sobbing as we freewheeled down a gentle, smoothly surfaced tarmac path. It genuinely could not have been more cycle-friendly, but she was adamant it was torture.

We eventually caught Rachel up (she and Ludo waited for us), and we stayed together for a mile or so. Just before we reached the halfway point, we pulled over to the side of the trail to eat some pasties that we had bought in Portreath. After a few minutes, Rachel suggested she and Ludo get a head start, as it was supposedly all downhill for the second half.

'Yeah, we'll catch you up,' I said. 'They'll be no stopping us after these pasties. Isn't that right, Kitty?'

Kitty scowled at me.

'Ok, have fun. I'll see you in a bit,' said Rachel, eager to escape the family conflict for a while.

When we finished our lunch, we packed up our things and got ready to leave. Layla and Kitty set off first, and Leo and I took up the rear.

'My bike feels weird,' said Leo. 'It's all wobbly.'

I looked down at his back tyre which was splayed across the gravel.

'Oh. You've got a flat tyre.'

I called after Layla and Kitty, but they were already too far ahead of us. Leo waited with his bike while I raced ahead to catch up with Layla and Kitty to tell them to wait while we fixed Leo's puncture.

Thankfully, I had a puncture repair kit with me so was confident we would be up and running in no time. I took off the tyre, located the source of the leak (the two-inch thorn protruding from the tyre was a clue) and sealed the hole with a patch. Then, as I tried to inflate the tyre, the pump came apart in my hands. And not in the kind of way that looked like it would ever pump again.

We had seen the occasional cyclist pass us while we ate, but now that we needed someone, we were all alone. We were also still in the midst of a global pandemic and I didn't want to make people feel uncomfortable by asking to borrow their pump and getting my suspiciously Covidy hands all over it.

'You should tell Mummy we have been delayed,' said Layla.

'Good idea,' I said, pulling out my phone. 'Oh. There's no signal.'

'Shall me and Kitty cycle ahead to try and catch her up?'

'No, I think we should all stay together. Just in case something happens to you or your bikes as well.'

I then remembered a little can of CO_2 that I had bought for emergency tyre inflation during my Ironman six years earlier. I had never used it. I had not even seen it in years. But sure enough, it was still squashed into the crevasses of my saddlebag. It was a little rusty, but worth a shot.

I nervously screwed the adaptor onto the canister, half expecting the thing to explode in my hand as I did so, but to my relief it seemed to lock into place. I then cautiously pressed the adaptor onto the tyre's valve and to my surprise it gave a big hiss.

'Get in!' I shouted.

'Is it working?' asked Leo.

'I think so. It seems to be inflating.'

I gave the tyre a little squeeze, and sure enough, there was some resistance.

'But how can a tiny little thing like that have enough air in to fill that massive bike tyre?' asked Layla.

'Because it's compressed air. Basically, this little thing has got loads of air squashed really tightly into a tiny little bottle.'

'That doesn't make any sense,' said Kitty. 'You can't squash that much air into something so small.'

'Just you wait,' I said, giving the tyre another little squeeze. Just as I did so, the hissing of the canister changed pitch, and then changed again, fizzling out into a gentle puff. And then nothing.

'Oh, it turns out you were right. There wasn't enough air to fill the whole tyre.'

'What do we do now?' said Leo.

'I think there's enough air in it for you to get back to the van. You might just not be as speedy as before.'

'Good!' said Kitty. 'He kept cycling off and leaving me behind.'

Our mechanical pitstop had taken nearly half an hour, but we were eventually up and running. With no pump and an empty CO_2 canister, I just had to hope that there were no more flat tyres. It had been a miracle that my fragile road bike had survived 20 miles of off-road cycling so far.

I eventually got a phone signal and was able to call Rachel to tell her about our delay, and a few miles later we found her and Ludo sitting in some woods by the side of the trail.

The scenery of the Cornish Coast to Coast was even better than I expected. It is very different to the coastal areas of Cornwall I was used to, and changes rapidly from stretches of woodland, through dusty old quarries, to empty farm tracks and nature reserves. Most people seem to begin at either end and then cycle a few miles out and back, so the section in the middle was almost deserted.

Our ride got even more eventful a few minutes later. Leo was cycling up ahead when I heard him skid in the gravel and I looked up to see him diving sideways off his bike before it toppled to the ground.

'A snake! A snake!' he shrieked.

I pulled up alongside him and sure enough, a large adder was slithering across the path inches from Leo's front wheel.

'I almost ran it over!' he said between sobs. 'It hissed at me and its head rose up as though it was going to bite me.'

'That sounds very scary. I think it's just a harmless grass snake,' I lied, as we watched the adder slowly disappear into the undergrowth. Rachel held on tightly to Ludo's lead and thankfully, he didn't seem to notice it.

'I don't want to cycle anymore,' said Leo. 'What if it happens again?'

'Don't worry. That was incredibly rare. I've been cycling all my life and I don't think I've ever nearly cycled over a snake. It won't happen again.'

The path got a lot busier the closer we got to the end in Devoran, with dozens of families, couples and individuals out enjoying the bright spring weather.

Kitty managed her first smile of the day a mile from the end when we turned a corner and were greeted with an honesty sweet stall set up at the side of the trail raising money for a local charity. And we had no more encounters with snakes, so the ride ended with smiles on everyone's faces.

FIVE

A few years ago, I signed Rachel up for her first ever marathon without her knowing. Since then, I have bought her and I places in various marathons as her Christmas present, including weekends in Barcelona, Rome and Paris. With overseas travel still uncertain and volatile, I played it safe for 2021 with a local event. I had, however, upped the stakes with the distance. This time I signed us up for a very hilly, off-road 100km running race. When I gave it to Rachel for Christmas, she had been oddly excited.

The East Devon Round had seemed like an exciting prospect to me, too, until a week before the race. It had always been the event in the future that would most likely get cancelled because of Covid. And if it did go ahead, it would no doubt be a fun and eventful way to spend a day. Now that it was a week away - and going ahead as planned - I felt extremely nervous. 100 kilometres! Sixty-two miles! With nearly 10,000 feet of climbing! How were we supposed to complete that?

It was May the 1st and after a fairly miserable winter, there had been a couple of weeks of beautiful sunshine, hinting we were entering summer. When we stepped outside of our house at 4.30am on the morning of the East Devon Round, however, there was a thick layer of frost on the car windscreen. Heavy frost in May is quite unusual, but it was in-keeping with the unpredictable nature of the weather that we would experience for the rest of the day.

We drove to the start of the race in the village of Offwell near Honiton in East Devon and arrived in plenty of time for the start. This was our first event since Race the Light just before Christmas 2020.

There were fewer than 100 people taking part, with some just running the first 50km. To help with social distancing, we set off in groups of six at two-minute intervals. We began our race at 6.15am, about half an hour after sunrise. Despite the early morning frost at home, the sky was blue, and it promised to be a beautiful day.

Two days before the East Devon Round, Rachel realised her running backpack was too small to carry all the things on the required kit list, let alone any extra food and water. During both of her previous ultras - the EnduranceLife South Devon Ultra and the Ridgeway 40 - her backpack had been far too small, and I ended up squashing a lot of her food and water into my bag. Somehow between those races and this one, she had forgotten that her bag was completely useless. This time, rather than getting me to carry all of our stuff, she bought a new backpack. One you could actually fit things into. It was refreshing for me to just be carrying my own food and water for a change.

Alasdair, the race director, and his team had done an incredible job of plotting the route. Almost all of it was off road on a combination of footpaths, bridleways, green lanes and private land that we had been allowed access to for the race.

After about two miles, we found ourselves running through a stunning bluebell wood. We stopped to let a runner pass us and then followed on behind. He looked familiar, but I couldn't place him. Rachel began chatting to him about the bluebells as we continued running. Our pace seemed to have picked up considerably, and I was struggling to keep up. Rachel continued chatting - mostly about bluebells - until we eventually reached a stile and by the time we had both climbed it, the other runner had thankfully disappeared up the path. It was at this point I realised where I had seen him. He had finished third in last year's East Devon Round and was also a regular podium finisher at some other races we had attended. I told Rachel who he was.

'Oh bloody hell,' she panted. 'I wish you'd remembered earlier. I'm knackered now.'

We reached a river crossing where the bridge was fenced off and heavy machinery parked up next to it. The bridge was in the process of being replaced and the structure didn't yet stretch all the way to the other side. Our map showed that this was where we were supposed to cross, so Rachel and I (and a few other runners who blindly followed us) bypassed the fence, carefully walked the section of the bridge that was there, and then jumped the final few feet onto the muddy bank. We then met some other runners who had found a fully intact bridge just a few metres further up the river.

As we slowed to a walk up a hilly field before Checkpoint 2, I checked my phone and found a message from my mum.

I think the man behind you is called Roger.

I had sent her the link to the live GPS tracking for the race, and she was obviously keeping tabs on us. By the time I read the message, there were about five or six of us running fairly close together, but there was one guy who had been near us for the last half an hour.

'Excuse me,' I said. 'Is your name Roger?'

He looked a little startled.

'Er... yes. I'm Roger.'

'Hi Roger. Nice to meet you. My mum just sent me a message saying that the bloke behind us was called Roger.'

He laughed, and looked relieved that I wasn't a weirdo stalker. Just the son of a weirdo stalker.

'Have you ever run 100k before?' asked Rachel.

'No, I've never done anything like this before. I'm completely out of my comfort zone.'

'You're doing really well,' I said.

I took a mid-run selfie of Rachel and me with Roger and sent it to my mum with the caption, *Roger our new BFF.*

Roger was wearing the East Devon Round 2021 souvenir t-shirt that we had been sent a week before the race. Rachel refused to even try hers on, believing it would somehow jinx the race.

We were also sent a commemorative neck buff, too, and Rachel would not even take hers out of the packet. I agreed that it was tempting fate to wear the event t-shirt to race in, but the buff would come in handy as we were required to wear a face mask at the start of the race and when at each of the checkpoints, so I decided to run with mine around my neck to use as a makeshift face covering. It was always in the back of my mind that using the commemorative neck buff would unleash some curse and cause a DNF.

It was a stunning route and so peaceful and quiet. At one point we were running along a footpath in a wood, the next we emerged into the town of Axminster. Minutes later, we were back in the countryside again.

We got a little lost as we entered Lyme Regis. We were following the paper map they had provided us with, and other runners were following GPS versions of the route they had downloaded onto their watches. Both routes differed slightly, but it didn't matter because the checkpoint was located by the beach and it is very difficult to lose the sea.

About seven miles of the route followed the South West Coast Path from Lyme Regis to Axmouth. Having run several marathons and ultramarathons along stretches of the South West Coast Path, a paltry seven miles would be a doddle. We had been warned by the race director that it was a particularly tough stretch, but I felt like I had run along some pretty tough sections of the coast path and thought it would unlikely cause any problems. How hard could it be? I was actually a little disappointed it was only a seven-mile section.

As we set off up the steps from Lyme Regis, I realised perhaps I had underestimated this stretch of coast path. From the seafront, the steps climbed relentlessly up the hillside into the woods. The path eventually levelled slightly and we could begin running again. We passed a sign warning that the terrain was difficult and the walking arduous. It also stated that there was no access to the sea or inland along this stretch, which basically meant there was no escape.

The next seven miles were some of the toughest we had ever run. I say run, but although we tried to run as much of it as possible, our average speed along this section was little quicker than walking pace. The path rollercoastered up and down, twisting its way through the trees. The surface was a tangle of exposed tree roots, rocks and mud, making it feel like a seven-mile obstacle course.

This area is a National Nature Reserve and has a unique history. On Christmas Eve 1839, a landslip began after weeks of heavy rain. By Boxing Day, 800 acres of farmland and gardens had slipped towards the sea, creating a vast chasm between it and the cliffs. This drastic change in geology created a humid micro climate that has allowed flora and fauna to flourish. Over 400 species of wildflower have been recorded in the Undercliffs (as they became known) and there is a diverse range of wildlife, too. Due to many non-native species of plants formerly growing in people's gardens, and the abundance of birds and other animals, the area feels like a tropical rainforest. It has gained the very appropriate nickname 'the jungle'. Despite how challenging it was, the Undercliffs was an incredible place to experience.

Midway through the jungle, we met Roger again. He wasn't as chirpy as when we last saw him. We walked with him for a while and he said he was just going to take it easy for a while and would catch us up.

My mum sent a message a few hours later.

Is Roger ok? His tracker hasn't moved for the last few hours.

'I hope he's ok,' said Rachel. 'See, I told you it was dangerous wearing a souvenir t-shirt during the actual race.'

'I'm having second thoughts about this neck buff now.'

Despite being on the coast path during this entire stretch, we only had a couple of brief glimpses of the sea. Our view was obstructed by the density of the vegetation and because long stretches of the path are in the chasm. The path occasionally teased us by opening up onto a headland, where it became wider and smoother, making us think we were over the worst of it, only for it to descend deep into the jungle again.

If it hadn't been for the fact that we weren't even halfway through our 100km, I would have been happy to spend more time in the Undercliffs. But it was a mighty relief to emerge eventually onto a golf course and then descend to the tarmac at Axmouth where we met a well-stocked feed station, full of crisps, sandwiches, ginger cake and sweets. The feed stations had a Covid policy in place, which meant these buffets were served by the marshals and we could point to what we wanted and have a plate made up for us. It was all extremely civilised and we felt very well looked after.

Rachel and I had both been in pretty good spirits all morning, considering we were running 100km. Rachel's mood changed dramatically just before we reached the halfway point at Blackbury Camp. We joined a footpath that took the direct route straight up the hillside at a gradient that must have been at least 30%.

'Oh god, I feel awful,' said Rachel.

'What's wrong?'

'I've got a pounding headache. And I feel exhausted.'

'We have almost covered 50km. It's not really surprising.'

'What if I've got Covid?'

'I don't think you've got Covid.'

'But what if I have?'

'Then you're doing even more remarkably.'

'What if I die?'

'It's just a hill. You are being very dramatic.'

She went very quiet, which is her tell-tale sign that she's not enjoying it.

As the path crested the top of the hill, we followed a track for a few minutes until we met a much needed feed station and Rachel perked up a bit. We gorged on ginger cake and flapjacks.

'How are you feeling now?'

'A lot better, thanks.'

'That's good. Who knew ginger cake and flapjack was a cure for Covid?'

We had been warned of a couple of last-minute route changes, brought on by previously supportive landowners withdrawing their consent on the day before the race on the grounds of not wanting to risk Covid entering their land. This had proved a logistical nightmare for the race organisers who had already marked out the course. Instead, large Xs were spray-painted onto the road surface, with arrows redirecting us a different way.

We circumnavigated a large sports field twice, trying to find the exit, only for another runner to tell us we needed to crawl through a barbed-wire fence. It later transpired that this fence had not been there during the early morning race-recce, and a landowner had taken pretty drastic steps to stop runners bringing Covid into their woodland.

As we ran in circles around the sports field, it had begun to hail. It is very rare for it to hail in May in southern England. And it wasn't just a brief shower. The hail continued for some time and settled on the ground like snow.

We still had a few hours of daylight left and it was quite mild, so Rachel and I ran through the hail in our t-shirts, hoping we would dry off before it got too cold at night.

An hour or so later, having dried off after the earlier hail, it began to hail again. This time much harder. With sunset less than two hours away, we pulled our jackets from our bags to try to keep warm. But by the time we put them on, our t-shirts were already soaked through. When the hail eventually stopped, I made the decision to take off my jacket in the hope that my t-shirt would dry during the last couple of hours of daylight. Rachel decided to keep her jacket on. It was a decision she would deeply regret later that night.

I received another message from my mum.

Roger's tracker still hasn't moved. It's been four hours. I'm worried about him.

I was a little worried about Roger too, but there didn't seem to be much we could do now. Presumably, those in charge of the tracking would have noticed. I told one of the marshals at a feed station that my mum was worried about Roger. They said they would pass the message on.

I checked the race results the next day, and Roger never made it onto the list of finishers. But he was also not listed as retired or DNF. According to the tracking information, Roger is still out on the course somewhere in the Undercliffs.

I sent the race organiser an email to check on Roger and he replied to tell me that Roger had indeed finished and there had been some issue with his GPS device being buried too deep in his backpack. My mum was mightily relieved.

After about 60km, our route left the public footpaths and passed up through another bluebell wood on private land. This section was new to the route and was introduced to showcase the bluebells. They were incredible, but the walk up to the top of the woods was one of the toughest of the day.

'Hi there. How are you doing?' I said to a runner who passed us when the path levelled out at the top.

'Yeah, good guys. How are you? FUCKING WANKER!' he muttered.

I was a little startled, but thought he must have just had a strange sense of humour.

'We're doing alright thanks. Not too long to go.'

'Yeah, keep going, you're doing well,' he said and continued to pull ahead of us. 'FUCKING SHITTY WANKERS!' he added.

'Did you hear that guy?' I said to Rachel. She didn't respond.

'Rachel? Did you hear that guy?'

'Sorry, what did you say?' she said, removing her woolly hat and headband that were covering her ears.

'That guy swore at us. He called us fucking wankers. Actually, I think he called us fucking shitty wankers.'

'No, I don't think he did, George. Why would he do that?'

A couple of minutes later, we passed a single glove lying in the middle of the path, presumably dropped by a runner ahead of us. I picked it up with the plan to leave it at the next feed station. Another minute or so later, we saw the sweary man running back towards us.

'Did you drop a glove?' I called.

'Yes, I did.'

'Here you go.'

'Thanks so much. I really appreciate it,' he said, taking the glove from me. 'FUCKING WANKER SHIT FUCK!'

He turned and began running up the path ahead of us again.

'See!' I whispered to Rachel. 'I told you!'

'Told me what?'

'He called me a fucking wanker shit fuck. Maybe he has Tourette's?'

Rachel had her hat and headband down again.

'I think you've gone mad, George.'

Twenty minutes later, we rounded a corner to find the same man crouched at the side of the path.

'Are you ok?' asked Rachel.

'I've broken my watch charger. It's almost out of battery, so I need to charge it with my battery pack. FUCKING SHITTY FUCK FUCK!'

I looked at Rachel with my 'see, I told you' eyes. She replied with her 'maybe I was wrong to doubt you' eyes.

'It works if I hold the lead really carefully like this, and then carry the battery pack in my other hand. I'm going to have to run like this for a while. FUCKITY SHIT WANKER!'

Again, he skipped off ahead of us, delicately using both hands to charge his watch whilst running.

We met him again a while later. He was no longer carrying his watch, but this time was having issues with a drinking bottle. He had filled his bottle with coke from a feed station, but the momentum of his running had caused the drink to fizz and the pressure had blown the seal off his bottle, spouting sticky cola everywhere.

'FUCKING SHITTY DRINKING BOTTLE!' he shouted, but I'm not sure whether this was his Tourette's or anger at his run of bad luck and his fucking shitty drinking bottle.

This time, he didn't disappear off and we walked with him up another steep wooded hill. He told us he had completed 196 marathons and ultramarathons, including several 100-mile races. 80km into the East Devon Round, he ranked it harder than any of his 100-milers. But given his bad luck with the lost glove, broken charger and fucking shitty drinking bottle, it's not surprising.

I wore my barefoot shoes for the East Devon Round. I had worn them for almost all of my runs since the beginning of 2020, so it seemed stupid to change to something else for a longer run. A couple of runners questioned my choice at the start line and seemed a little dubious about whether it was a wise idea.

12 hours into the race and I was beginning to think that they might be right. The shoes had been fine all day on the off-road sections, but we reached a road for the first time in hours and as we ran down a steep section, my feet were taking a pounding from the tarmac. They felt very sensitive and uncomfortable and I craved something with a bit more cushioning. Presumably everyone's feet would feel like they've taken a pounding after 12 hours running?

I woke the next morning with no blisters and no foot or leg pain, so I think that must surely go down as a win for the barefoot shoes.

As we were running down this road towards the penultimate feed station in the village of Luppitt, a car pulled up alongside of us.

'Hello strangers,' said a voice.

Two friends of ours - Cath and Marissa - had driven nearly two hours from home to come and cheer us on. They had been following us on the GPS site and happened to arrive on one of the very few accessible parts of the course at the same time as us. I hope Roger's friends didn't go to try and surprise him in the middle of the jungle.

It was really touching to see them both, and Rachel and I got a little choked up. They went ahead and parked up at the next feed station, which we ran straight past without noticing and Cath and Marissa had to run out into the road to call us back.

The feed stations during the East Devon Round were incredible. And they got better, the further into the race we went, knowing that food becomes more and more a priority to the runners.

The penultimate feed station at Luppitt was particularly special with cups of hot chunky soup, pizza, sandwiches, wraps and crisps. I was feeling pretty good, so ate most of the things on offer. I had never eaten soup mid-run, or even remotely desired it, but it was a particular highlight.

It was wonderful to see Cath and Marissa, and we were hugely appreciative of them coming all that way just to cheer us on. Your emotions do crazy things during endurance events. You become far more sensitive to acts of kindness. Having friends spend most of their day coming to see you for 10 minutes is a massive deal.

You also seem to form strangely deep emotional attachments to people you've never met before (and will probably never see again). You can have a very brief conversation with another runner and you experience an intense level of connection you might not even get from people you've known for years. 50 miles into a run, you have a surprising amount in common with the runners you see. Both of you decided at some point that this would be a fun way to spend a day, and you both chose to pay money to enter it. And after countless hours on your feet, many miles already covered but many more still to go, you most likely feel on a very similar physical and mental plane to them too.

This emotional attachment isn't just limited to other runners. Even people manning the feed stations, marshals, and random supporters suddenly feel like close friends. You are at your most vulnerable, stripped of any pretence and artifice, and you feel a powerful level of kinship to those helping you along your way.

One such runner was Katie. Katie was still in her twenties, but had a CV of events longer than most experienced competitors three times her age. We met up with her several times between kilometres 75 and 85. She would then skip nimbly off ahead, putting all her faith in the GPS route which she had downloaded onto her watch. It turned out the GPS route had its limitations and we kept spotting her on the wrong side of hedgerows, while we followed our trusty paper map. Her family was out to support her and she met them at strategic points and then caught up with us a few minutes later.

From the feed station at Luppitt, Rachel and I climbed steeply up onto the long, ridge-shaped Hartridge Hill. A lively American runner overtook us. We were over 85km into a race and he was skipping along like he was just out for a 5km. We got chatting to him and he told us how there was a 100 mile race he had finished in the Rockies in Colorado. There was over 30,000 feet of elevation and it had taken him 40 hours to complete. He enjoyed it so much he had done it five more times. The East Devon Round was just the equivalent of a short, easy 5km run for him. We wished him luck and he skipped off ahead.

Dumpdon Hill was our final significant challenge for the day. Dumpdon Hill sits just outside Honiton and is the location of an Iron Age hillfort. We unintentionally timed our visit to its summit just as the sun was setting, and were rewarded with stunning views of the Otter Valley and surrounding countryside, with the backdrop of the last of the evening light.

Both Rachel and I were in good spirits, knowing we only had about eight miles to go. We were keen to get off the hill before it got too dark. During the steep descent, Rachel's quads seized up badly. I knew we were very close to the final feed station and was eager to get there as soon as possible. It was a gentle downhill half-mile across fields all the way there, but it took us a very long time to reach it. The temperature plummeted once the sun had dipped below the horizon.

Unlike the other feed stations, which were all outdoors, this one was in a village hall where we got to stand for a few minutes under the warm glow of electric heaters. Rachel went to use the toilet and I stuffed my face with sweets and a drank a couple of glasses of coke. I had avoided too much sugar (apart from the ginger cake and flapjack at halfway), fearing I would suffer the consequences of an energy crash. With about seven miles to go, my standards had slipped and I shovelled Haribo into my mouth like I was preparing for hibernation.

A couple of other runners arrived and both tried to use the toilet, but it was still occupied by Rachel. Ten minutes passed, and I thought I better go check on her.

'Yes, I'm ok,' she said. 'I'll be out in a minute.'

She emerged five minutes later, embarrassed to find that others had been waiting to use the toilet.

'I was worried about you,' I said. 'Were you ok in there?'

'Yes, I just put on some more clothes and then just sat down for a while.'

'Did you fall asleep on the toilet?'

'No! Of course I didn't. I was only in there a couple of minutes.'

'You were in there at least 15 minutes.'

'Oh. Huh. I'm pretty sure I didn't fall asleep.'

Katie was also at this feed station and had changed into waterproof trousers and a thicker jacket.

'Do you guys mind if I run to the finish with you?' she said. 'Navigating in the dark is not so appealing on my own.'

'Of course not, that would be great,' I said.

'I'm going to be very slow, I'm afraid,' said Rachel. 'It's likely to be more of a walk.'

'That's fine with me,' said Katie. 'I'm in no hurry at all.'

Rachel's legs were in a bad way and even walking was proving to be a challenge. She never once considered stopping, though. More worryingly, she was also extremely cold. We had been far too slow to react to the earlier hail and didn't put on our waterproofs until we were already soaked through. When the hail stopped, I had taken my jacket off and the final two hours of sunlight had dried my clothes by the time it got dark. Rachel had kept her coat on and her t-shirt was still soaking wet beneath her jacket. I gave her the spare base layer I was carrying, and she wore a spare pair of my socks over her hands, but she was still shivering uncontrollably as she walked.

After a few navigational fails with her GPS throughout the day, we were extremely grateful to have Katie and her watch with us once it was dark. A series of ribbons tied to trees and gates marked the route. Most of the day had been spent running from ribbon to ribbon. On a couple of occasions in the last few miles, however, we entered a field marked with a ribbon, but there was no way of telling where the field exit was. Without Katie, Rachel and I would have had to follow the field perimeter until we found the next ribbon. Thankfully, Katie's watch could guide us the correct way.

With less than two miles to go, we caught sight of torchlight up ahead. There looked to be three head torches, all heading in the same direction as us, but the three runners were bunched strangely close together. As we got closer, we realised the middle person was being supported by those on either side. It was the man who had finished third the previous year, who Rachel had chatted to about bluebells earlier in the race. He was struggling with injuries, stomach issues and extreme lethargy.

We asked if there was anything we could do to help, but the two people with him - family members who had come to cheer him on - said they would stay with him until the finish.

At one point, he had been almost two hours ahead of us. He ended up finishing another 45 minutes behind. It showed extraordinary commitment for him to continue to the finish line despite being in such a bad way. And it was astonishing to see the help and support (in this case, literally) of his family to allow him to achieve his goal and avoid the DNF.

It also made Rachel feel a little better about her own situation.

Our watches ticked over 100km. This had been the mystical figure we had been aiming for. Throughout the day, all of our calculations of how far we had left to run were based on the race being 100km. And here we were, in the middle of a field, with no sign of civilisation in any direction.

'Er, I'm afraid my watch says we still have 2.5km to go,' said Katie.

This was incredibly demoralising, as an additional 2.5km seemed a ridiculously long way.

Rachel gave an enormous sigh.

The GPS trackers we were carrying had an emergency distress button on them. I was tempted to press mine. We had done 100km. That is what we had agreed to.

'Right, that's it. We're done. We signed up for 100km. I'm not walking another metre. Send in the helicopters. I'm outta here.'

But of course we didn't press the button and plodded on.

The final 10km took us almost 2.5 hours. With about half a kilometre to go, we reached a stile at the edge of a field.

'Oh, this is so cruel,' said Katie. 'I'm honestly not sure if I'll be able to get over this.'

She climbed precariously onto the stile and then had to use both hands to lift her leg over the gate. It was at this point, when she had both legs astride the stile, that I noticed there was no fence attached to one side of the stile. So I just walked around it.

'Oh my god,' said Katie. 'I can't believe I just did that.'

Rachel breathed a sigh of relief and stepped around it too.

The finish area was lined with beautiful fairy lights. Most people had gone home or were tucked up in their tents pitched in the nearby sports field. We crossed the line 16 hours and 26 minutes after we started. It was a peaceful and serene end to the race. Katie met up with her boyfriend and gave him a big hug. Rachel and I gave each other a hug.

'Well done! What can I get you? Beer? Tea? Pizza? Sandwich?' asked Alasdair, the race director, with surely the most personal post-race welcome we will ever receive.

'I would l-l-l-love a c-c-c-cup of t-t-t-tea,' said Rachel, through chattering teeth.

'Just water for me, please.'

'Would you like a couple of beers to take with you for later?'

'Wow, yes please.'

He returned with the tea, water and beers, and also some elasticated race belts that he gave to us as an impromptu prize for being the first husband and wife team to cross the finish line. I think we were probably the only (and therefore last) husband and wife team, too. But surviving 100km with your partner felt like an impressive achievement. Only 60 runners took part, and when we checked the results later, we discovered we weren't even the fastest Rachel and George.

The final two hours in the dark had been a brand new experience for us. It was great fun and strangely exhilarating, but it made navigating so much more difficult. Some runners were out for five hours longer than us, meaning seven hours of navigating in the dark. It's possible several of those hours were spent trying to get over that final pointless stile.

It was a ten-minute drive to the hotel and as I parked up in the car park, Rachel didn't look in a good way. There was a kerb to negotiate between the van and the hotel entrance, and she had a brief moment where she began to cry in the car park.

'What's the matter?' I asked.

'I feel so awful.'

'I'm not surprised. We've just run 100km. In fact, more than 100km'

'I know, but I feel REALLY awful.'

'Well, we are at the hotel now. You can have a nice bath and then go to bed.'

'I don't think I can get to the hotel room. Do you think I need to go to hospital?'

'No, I think you need to go to bed.'

She had another big sob when I helped her over the kerb, and then we staggered into the empty hotel lobby. The receptionist looked a little concerned but handed over our keycard with no questions. Once up in the room, I filled the bath for Rachel and made her another cup of tea.

'I'm going to nip over to the 24-hour garage across the road and buy some beers and some food. What would you like to eat?'

'Oh god, nothing for me, thanks. Maybe just a fruit salad if they have something. But I don't think I'll be able to eat it until morning.'

'Are you sure you don't want anything now? It might make you feel better.'

'No, I don't think I could.'

I looked around the room for the keycard and then realised we had only been given one. And it was currently inserted in the slot on the wall that activated all the lights in the room. I needed the key, as the hotel had a couple of security doors between the lobby and our room.

'Er... will you be alright if I leave you in the dark for a few minutes?'

'Why?'

'Because the keycard is powering the lights, and I need it if I go to the garage.'

'Do you have to go to the garage?'

'Er... no, I guess I don't have to.'

I had a choice. I could either leave Rachel, who was in a pretty bad state, in complete darkness, while I made a selfish trip to get beer and snacks. Or I could do the right thing and make do with a cup of tea and the free biscuits in the hotel room.

'I'll be as quick as I can,' I said, pulling the card from the slot and plunging her into darkness.

She was still alive when I returned and feeling a little better. The big bag of crisps, pasta salad, two scotch eggs, bar of chocolate and the two cans of beer I bought from the garage made me feel much better, too.

On the drive home the following morning, Rachel spent a considerable time deconstructing her race statistics on Strava. She has always been quite competitive with me, but if we run a race side by side, it's not really possible to compare stats as we completed each mile at exactly the same pace. There is still one distinguishing factor that can be analysed. Heart rate.

'Ha, get in!' she said. 'My average heart rate for the entire race was lower than yours!'

A lower average heart rate suggests a higher level of fitness.

'Really? How different?'

'Enough to be significant. Yours was 134bpm. Mine was only 128bpm.'

'Wow, impressive. Well done.'

'You sound sarcastic.'

'Not at all. Although, you need to remember that your watch was charging in your backpack for about an hour. Probably at the same time your heart rate was off the scale. And also, your heart had pretty much stopped beating by the end, so it's no wonder it was so low.'

'You're such a dick.'

SIX

In the days following our sign up to the Royal Marines Iron Challenge (RMIC), a group of 11 local friends decided to take part. My friend Tim, who I ran with fairly regularly, went from being 5% interested to 95% once he heard everyone else had signed up. An hour later, he had paid his entry fee and set up a group chat for us all. His opening message said: *Welcome all. Who'd have thought most of us hadn't even heard of this event a week ago?! Thanks Sophie.*

Most had taken part in a half-iron distance before, but out of the 11, I was the only one to have attempted a full. Somehow, this made me the most experienced, and supposedly most knowledgeable. The group then took the piss for several months about me being an expert on everything triathlon. I told them my *Operation Ironman* book had all been a lie and none of it had ever happened.

The truth is, we were all equally unprepared for this mammoth event and there was a wonderful, shared sense of camaraderie to be taking part with equally naive friends.

The race directors of the RMIC also set up a dedicated group chat. This was the first big event they had organised together, and they were more pumped than anyone. This was their baby, and they were desperate to make it an enjoyable experience for all involved.

Several times a week, they arranged swim training sessions at Blackpool Sands beach, which was to be the location of the swim and the race HQ on the day. Rachel attended a few of these sessions and I managed to use childcare as an excuse to get out of going. We could have easily taken the children with us, but I was secretly intimidated by swimming with others. Especially when many of them were Royal Marines. I think that was the main reason Rachel was so keen to go to these sessions.

Rachel's swimming improvement trajectory had been pretty rapid, heading on a steep upward curve. Mine had plateaued years ago. I had learned how to swim front crawl while training for my first Ironman six years earlier, but my speed and stamina had made little improvement since. On the few occasions Rachel and I went out and swam together, she would now slowly edge ahead of me.

Rachel's cycling had come on leaps and bounds, too. She was regularly up before dawn to take advantage of the quiet roads with her friends Kate and Claire. Although their cycling had improved considerably, Rachel's bike maintenance skills were still lacking. On one occasion, Claire got a flat tyre midway through a bike ride with Rachel. They replaced the inner tube like I had showed Rachel many times before and then attempted to inflate it with the small pump I had bought her to use in such a situation. But they couldn't get the pump to work. For some very strange reason that I still don't understand, they thought it would be a good idea to determine whether the issue was with the pump or the inner tube. To do this, Rachel deliberately let out all the air from one of her tyres. Again, they couldn't get the pump to work. And now they had two flat tyres. The issue wasn't with the pump or the inner tubes. It was with them.

They watched a couple of YouTube videos and half an hour later had two partially inflated tyres and were able to cover the remaining miles to get home.

Rachel was pretty dedicated to her training. She had a few minor injuries and a few setbacks, but she was more than ready. Training for an event such as an iron-distance triathlon can be quite a selfish endeavour. There's a lot of time involved and if you are in a relationship and have kids and responsibilities, it often means your partner has to pick up a lot of the slack. Having both of us take part relieved all of this guilt.

In the build-up to my previous Ironman (have I mentioned I did an Ironman?), I obviously felt very nervous and anxious about the event. But I didn't feel any pressure or expectation to do well. It had been a self-imposed challenge that I had set myself as a means of trying to get fit after my surgery. Completing the Ironman would always just be a bonus. Nobody expected me to do well. In fact, many friends and family would have probably preferred I didn't take part. So there was no weight of expectation on me at all.

It felt very different preparing for the RMIC. This time, I was supposedly the expert. This time I did have some weight of expectation. This time I did feel pressure to do well. DNF was not an option.

I had trained alone for my first Ironman. Because I was recovering from surgery, I just did what I could. I built up my fitness slowly and hoped it would be enough on the day. This time round the training took on a whole different level of importance.

It was all-consuming. For the months leading up to the RMIC, it was constantly on our minds. It would enter our thoughts as soon as we woke up and hang around there until we went to sleep that night, often reappearing in our dreams in different forms.

Our crew of 11 all followed each other on Strava, so we could each see how much (or little) everyone else was doing. Sometimes this was beneficial, as it provided a bit of motivation to get out there and do some training. But it also made you constantly feel like you weren't doing enough. There was always somebody cycling further, running faster, swimming more regularly.

There were even rumours of people out training in stealth mode. Going for runs and bike rides in secret and not uploading them publicly to Strava.

But the benefits of training as part of a group far outweighed the negatives. There was always someone to go for a swim, ride or run with. Always someone to provide words of advice or comfort. And training with others is so much more enjoyable than on your own. It felt less lonely. It felt like more of a shared experience.

SEVEN

One Sunday morning in May, I was playing football like I do most weekends. We take it in turns to go in goal, and ten minutes into the match I offered to do my stint.

One of our players erratically kicked the ball back to me. As it was a pass back, I wasn't allowed to handle the ball so tried to control it with my feet. I made a poor first touch and sent the ball up into the air. As one of the opposition strikers chased down the loose ball, I decided to try to head it clear. We both jumped at the same time and after heading it, I turned to protect myself. Unfortunately, the other player's momentum carried him (and his knee) through the air and crashed into the middle of my back. In that split second, it felt like one or two of the lower ribs in my back had broken.

The initial pain eased slightly after a few seconds, and was replaced with the feeling of being heavily winded. It was a few minutes before I could get my breath back. I stupidly played on, hoping that I would be able to run it off. I stayed in goal to see out the remaining hour or so of the match. The muscles in my back continued to spasm every time I moved or took a deep breath. I was unable to bend or reach upwards, so conceded three soft goals - including being lobbed twice. Thankfully, we won the match 4-3 and my team actually played better when I wasn't on the pitch.

I cycled the three miles home and then spent the rest of the day trying and failing to find a comfortable position to sit in.

The following morning, after dropping the kids at school, I went to the hospital and they confirmed I had broken a rib. It would take six weeks to heal and I should abstain from any strenuous exercise for the duration.

At the age of 42, this was my first official broken bone. I think I broke a toe once during my paper round and another playing football, but neither was confirmed. For a while, I thought that getting to 42 without breaking anything was a good achievement. I then worried that this was a sign that I'm getting old and more brittle and it could perhaps be the first of many.

Since my back surgery six years earlier, I had felt fairly invincible. I rarely thought about my surgery (despite going on about it all the time in my books) and did not feel any more vulnerable as a result. In the meantime, I had suffered plenty of injuries, aches and pains since. But all of those were minor tweaks or strains. Nothing that would have been made noticeably worse with activity.

A broken bone was different. It was an actual physical defect. It made me feel strangely fragile and vulnerable.

Getting in and out of the car was particularly painful. As was getting off the sofa. I couldn't sit comfortably in my desk chair, so got little writing done. I couldn't sleep very well at night. All in all, it wasn't an enjoyable experience.

It was a bit of a setback for my RMIC training. The event was still four months away, so there should be plenty of time to recover. I spoke to my cousin who had broken his rib a year earlier while skiing and it was still causing him problems. I hoped he was an extreme case, rather than the norm. I abstained from all exercise for the following three weeks to try to give it the best chance of healing.

It often felt like we were through the Covid pandemic and were making a return to normality. Then there would be another spike in cases and we were back where we were in 2020. There were countless mixed messages coming from the UK government. We should continue to stay at home, unless we couldn't stay at home. We should work from home, but we should return to our places of work. We shouldn't go to pubs and restaurants, but we should go to pubs and restaurants to eat out to help out. Parents were not allowed to attend children's sports days. But tens of thousands of people cramming in to watch football at Wembley was fine. Leo's football team had a tournament cancelled because it breached new Covid rules, but another one went ahead because it was called a 'football festival' instead.

During the first wave of the pandemic, there were no tests available. Now we all had cupboards full of lateral flow tests. With three children at two different schools, and Rachel teaching, we were testing several times a week. The children kept winding Rachel up by drawing a line on her test with a pen. She fell for it every single time.

There became a weight of social pressure to avoid getting Covid at crucial times: weddings, birthdays, holidays, events. There was an anxious wait each time to see if we were all still Covid free.

Rachel is two months older than me (as I like to remind her regularly), so for several weeks I would ask if her age group had got the call yet to have her vaccine. When she finally received a text inviting her to book an appointment, I had just two hours of bragging before my text arrived.

Rachel booked a spot later that week but I was due to drive Leo and three of his friends to a football tournament, sorry, I mean football festival, so didn't think it was wise to get jabbed the same day in case of any adverse reactions.

The vaccines seemed to make people more divisive than ever, with those pro-vaccine and those antivax. Even within those supporting the vaccine, there was even more division about the different brands of vaccine. There was a lot of talk in the news and amongst friends and family about the different vaccines and potential side effects.

'My friend's mum's brother's neighbour had the Pfizer vaccine and her hair turned green,' declared one.

'This guy I met had a friend who knew some girl who met a girl who had AstraZeneca and she could not turn left afterwards,' claimed another.

'You don't want Moderna. It's apparently mostly made out of pig semen and chip fat.'

Comparing vaccines and side effects became a strange obsession with the public. One friend of mine - who is usually liberally minded - claimed that AstraZeneca must be the better vaccine as British scientists created it and it was therefore obviously superior to all the others.

There was also an uncomfortable level of competition between countries about their vaccine rollout.

The UK are leading the world with their vaccine rollout! Get in! Let the rest of the world suffer! It felt so wrong.

I had my vaccine two days after Rachel. It was administered at the same venue, but I had a different brand.

'Ah, I think mine must be what they give to the younger people,' I said.

She didn't even bother responding.

EIGHT

After the Cornish Coast to Coast, Kitty swore she would never get on a bike ever again. I knew she wouldn't stick to this threat, but in the meantime, we made sure we got out for regular walks instead.

Walking became our go to activity at weekends or during the holiday. Having Ludo meant we had a commitment to get outside, whatever the weather.

We continue to head to Dartmoor regularly at weekends or during the school holidays. There is still plenty of moaning, but it's getting less as the children have grown to accept that this is the way it's going to be. After all, they were the ones who persuaded me to get a dog in the first place. They always feel good after completing these walks, even if they are not always enjoyable at the time.

One of our walks didn't get off to the best of starts. We reached a set of stepping stones over a stream, ten minutes after leaving the car park. For some reason, Kitty decided not to use the stepping stones and bizarrely removed her shoes instead. She tried to hand me one of her shoes, but let go of it before I had a hold and it fell into the water and swiftly drifted downstream. I then had to step into the water and wade after it while Kitty sobbed and moaned at 'stupid Daddy' for dropping her stupid shoe in the stupid stream.

I pointed out that maybe if the stupid shoe had stayed on her stupid foot then it wouldn't have ended up in the stupid stream. In her anger, she accidentally dropped her other shoe into the stream, so we each had two soaking wet feet less than a quarter of a mile into the walk.

Within half a mile, everyone else's feet were soggy too, as the recent rain had left parts of the path underwater and staying dry was impossible.

The day did improve. We traversed stretches of bleak open moor, crossed many rivers, either via stepping stones or wading, walked through ancient woodlands and had three incredible swims along the way. Dartmoor has thousands of footpaths spider-webbed all over the national park, but most are quite hard to follow. There is a right to roam across Dartmoor, so footpaths tend to be a rough guide, rather than a favoured route. But that is part of its appeal.

Leo did some geocaching using my phone to give him his brief technology hit, and despite being the middle of August and the height of tourist season, we saw less than a dozen people out walking on the moor. And half of those were two families who we passed twice, presumably doing the same walk as us but in reverse. One of the UK's most unspoilt areas and it's largely deserted.

The guidebook we were following said the walk was supposed to be six miles, but Dartmoor miles seem to be significantly longer than normal miles. My watch ticked over 9.5 miles by the time we reached the van, and Ludo must have walked at least twice that. The children wanted to do laps of the car park until my watch reached 10 miles. This was the furthest any of them had ever walked, and considering the hilly and muddy terrain, it was a brilliant achievement from all of them.

We picked up a Chinese takeaway on the way home and then ate dinner in front of a movie after a particularly memorable day. Even Layla seemed to enjoy it, although she refused to admit it.

NINE

There was an increase in activity in the group chat for the RMIC. Several Marines and former Marines had signed up to the challenge and there was a lot of military lingo bandied around. Phrases like *hoofing, goffers, threaders, gucci* and *wets and dits* got thrown around into the chat as part of normal conversation. Over time, the eleven of us civvies learned the meanings of these phrases. By the time of the event, we would pretty much be Royal Marines, too.

As part of their event preparation, and to commemorate the D-Day landings, they put on a 6km swim along the coast from the beach at Blackpool Sands, to the memorial for Operation Tiger at the village of Torcross.

Rachel was eager to take part. I was eager not to. But I knew I would regret it if she completed it and I didn't, so reluctantly agreed. That was long before I broke my rib. The D-Day swim was three weeks to the day after breaking it, so I assumed it would be an event I would have to miss.

To sort out the safety logistics of swimmers being spread out over 6km, we had to arrange our own kayak or

SUP safety support. We persuaded two friends - Cath and Abs - to join us. With the option of being rescued by my own personal support crew, I decided to give it a go. If my rib was too painful, I now at least had a means of escape.

Having completed a few longer swims, I was not too daunted by the distance of the D-Day swim. But that didn't make me any more excited about it. Plus, other than the Plymouth Breakwater Swim nearly six years previously, I had never swum more than a mile in the sea before. It would be Rachel's longest ever swim by some distance. The undulations of the waves, the salt water in the mouth, and the fear of what lurks beneath make it a very different prospect to swimming in a lake or river. Nausea and seasickness are very common.

Having kayak support meant we could bring food and water and have access to it whenever we wanted. Rachel didn't know what to expect, so packed a full picnic. She had crisps, sandwiches, energy bars, energy drinks and even some chocolate crepes. I knew from experience that eating and swimming is quite a hard combination. So my kayak had a bottle of water, a packet of crisps and a banana.

Conditions were perfect when we turned up at Blackpool Sands on the morning of the swim. There were just 17 of us taking part. Six from our group of eleven who would be taking part in the RMIC also took part in the D-Day swim. The other five sensibly decided it would likely put them off swimming completely.

Straining to get into my wetsuit was very painful, but once in, it seemed to provide some sort of support for my rib. Almost like I was wearing one of those body braces that doctors used to prescribe to people with back problems.

We were given a race briefing, provided with tow floats and tracking devices and we waded out into the water. There was a short countdown, and then we were off. Because of the small number of us taking part, there was a relatively calm and relaxed atmosphere. The sea was beautifully clear and calm and for a few short strokes, we could look down through the water at the sandy bottom, before it disappeared, and we were out into the open ocean.

Six kilometres is a long way to swim in the sea. I had completed the River Dart 10k three times (and had the gold hat to prove it), but that had been tide and current assisted. The river is a long series of sweeping bends, so there was never the daunting sight of being able to see how far we had left to swim. It was just a case of taking one bend at a time.

The D-Day swim was very different. As soon as we were out past the first headland, we could see our destination further down the coast. And it looked a bloody long way. I had run and cycled the length of the Slapton Line many times over the years, and it felt like a long way on foot or bike. Swimming it seemed ludicrous. Yet here we were, swimming the entire length of the Slapton Line.

The conditions were perfect. But that didn't make it any more pleasurable. It should have been brilliant. Except it was so bloody tedious. Rachel put her head down and kept making strokes. She breathed every three, looked up briefly to get her bearings every so often, but hardly ever broke her stroke. As hard as I tried, I seemed to be unable to go for more than 30 seconds without stopping. Partly because of the discomfort, but mostly because of boredom. Swimming is great when your head is above water. All the fun aspects disappear when your face is submerged throughout.

To make coming up for air even more tempting, Cath and Abs, our safety support, seemed to be having a lovely time, floating along on a calm, flat sea. It was much more enjoyable being above water chatting with them than with my head underwater, so I resorted to breaststroke for big chunks of the swim.

I wish I could get into the mindset of swimmers like Rachel who can put their head down and keep going. I've asked Rachel what she thinks about, and she's quite vague and just says, 'I just love looking at all the bubbles.'

It would be easy to blame my broken rib, but it didn't cause too many problems. There was the occasional short, sharp burst of pain if I twisted too much, or breathed too quickly. My lower back felt uncomfortable because of three weeks of inactivity. But that was nothing compared to the discomfort in my mind. I was desperate for it all to be over and almost hoped a shark would come and put me out of my misery.

At about the halfway point, I managed a sip of water and a bite of banana. I had brought them along, so felt I should at least have something. Rachel didn't even touch her extensive picnic.

Some swimmers opted to hug the shoreline. There were rumours you were less likely to encounter jellyfish. The disadvantage is the waves tend to be more prominent closer to shore. Others took a line extremely far out and probably ended up swimming an extra kilometre to get back to shore.

They had also warned us how cold we would feel after potentially 2.5 hours in the sea. Many of the swimmers wore balaclavas, two wetsuits, two swimming hats, neoprene gloves, booties, and several had opted for plastic marigold gloves - the kind used for washing dishes - on top of their other gloves. During the briefing, I stood there in just my thin wetsuit and single swim hat and felt very under-dressed.

We need not have worried. The sea temperature was fine and none of us felt cold. There were also, thankfully, no jellyfish sightings. We were out in the deep ocean and there's nothing to see underwater, thank god. I would regularly spook myself with my own air bubbles and sometimes my own hand, imagining I'd seen some deadly sea creature aiming for my face.

It got a little choppier for the last half an hour, but we eventually made it to the finish line after 2 hours and 22 minutes. I knew Rachel had been kindly holding back to wait for me and could have completed it much quicker.

As we staggered up the beach, I was shocked to see my mum and dad standing there. My parents have always shown an interest in my sporting activities and check results or ask how I got on, or stalk fellow competitors (poor Roger). But over the course of many years, countless marathons, triathlons and ultramarathons, they have never once been there at the finish line. I found it quite emotional.

Until I discovered they had been out on a long bike ride to Lidl to buy pastéis de nata (Portuguese custard tarts) and just so happened to be passing the beach at Torcross when they saw the swimmers emerging from the water. Still, it was very nice to see them.

The D-Day swim was a great confidence boost for all six of us taking part in the RMIC. At 6km, the D-Day swim was over 2km further than the swim leg of the triathlon. And as boring as I found it, it also dispelled some of the fear factor for me about swimming in the open sea.

At this point, we had not yet been informed about a crucial detail of the RMIC swim.

We would be entering the water about 1.5 hours before sunrise.

TEN

Leo finished primary school in July and would move on to secondary school in September. His SATS exams were cancelled because of the pandemic (much to the annoyance of Layla who had been through them a few years earlier), so he had a relatively relaxing end to his time at primary school.

Our last holiday abroad was in 2019 and we decided to stay in the UK for 2021 too. We had a few days camping with friends in the New Forest, but otherwise spent the summer holidays at home. We met up with my friend Damo (who claims his grandma invented banoffee pie), my sister and her family spent a couple of weeks down here in Devon, and Rachel's sister and family came down too.

Rachel's sister's family is currently undertaking an impressive challenge to climb the highest peaks in each county in England. Earlier in the year, we had joined them to climb Dunkery Hill, Somerset's highest peak. Then, during their holiday in Devon, we helped them tick off the highest peak in Devon - High Willhays (pronounced High Willies, which kept us all amused during the challenging walk).

It had been over two years since I had published a book. I had been blaming the extenuating circumstances of Covid. How long would I be able to use this excuse for?

In January 2020, way back when things were different, I began researching and writing a self-help book. It was supposed to be a light-hearted, tongue-in-cheek poke at the genre. But the more I read, and the more I wrote, the more serious (and hopefully useful) the tone became. And then Covid happened and reading all of these books for research became beneficial for keeping me sane.

In the meantime, I also began writing this *Did Not Finish* series. I had kept notes from all the events Rachel and I had taken part in for the last few years and decided to write them up. I got very little writing done during homeschooling, but after the children returned to school in March, I realised that I probably couldn't use the 'extenuating circumstances' excuse for too much longer. So I sat at my desk and got writing. By July, I had finished the first six and had them all ready to release over the summer.

My training for the RMIC had not been as thorough as I hoped, but I knew I was fitter than when I did my first Ironman. It had been a while since I had been on a long bike ride, so managed to squeeze in a couple of big solo rides to try to prepare for the day.

On one long ride in August, I foolishly set out on one of the hottest days of the year to cycle the perimeter of Dartmoor. I arrived at a bakery in Bovey Tracey in time for breakfast, put on my face mask and went in and bought some pastries and a coffee.

I stopped again in Moretonhamstead, but looked in my bike bag and there was no sign of my mask. I checked all my pockets and my saddlebag, but it wasn't there either. I was angry with myself for losing it. It must have fallen out and was littering the countryside, or strangling a bird in a bush somewhere. I was such an idiot. Masks were not compulsory at this stage of the pandemic, but most places still asked you to wear one. And the fact that I was bright red and covered in sweat made people look at me as though I had Covid, anyway.

I stuck my head inside a bakery and explained I didn't have a mask. The lady looked at me strangely and then told me she didn't mind me coming in without. It happened again in a bakery in Okehampton. The man behind the counter looked a little perplexed but told me they didn't mind me going in without a mask. I stopped again in Tavistock and Yelverton, and again bought food and drink without my mask.

The heat was relentless and it took me a long time to get home. Once finished, I went to unclip my helmet and the clasp got caught on something under my chin. It was my stupid face mask. It had been under my chin the entire time. I looked back at my photos of the day, which included several selfies, and my mask was extremely visible in all of them. The sun had been so bright I hadn't noticed while taking the photos.

It now became clear why all those in the shops and bakeries looked at me so oddly when I told them I didn't have a mask. Why did nobody tell me?

ELEVEN

On New Year's Day 2021, Rachel and I signed up for our first ever swimrun - The Rocky Horror Swimrun - scheduled to take place in September, later that year. Swimrun events began in Scandinavia and involve competitors island hopping by running across an island and then swimming to the next. The popularity has spread and events are popping up across the world. We persuaded three friends to join us, who were all possibly still drunk from New Year's Eve the night before, and full of hope and promise for the year to come.

Then the world turned to shit and everything got cancelled, including our swimrun event. We were all secretly relieved as we had signed up for the longer course, which comprised about 20 miles trail running and two miles of swimming. With the now far bigger concern of the Royal Marines Iron Challenge looming over us, we didn't think about the swimrun again.

Then at the very end of August in 2021 - 20 months after we originally signed up - Rachel and I received an email advising us of some last-minute details about the race. Last-minute details to a race we didn't even know was happening. Last-minute details to a race that was taking place in a week's time.

Our initial thoughts were that just two weeks before our iron-distance triathlon, it was too close and not worth the risk. 20 miles of running and swimming along the rugged South Devon coast would not only be extremely tiring but also fairly risky so soon before the RMIC.

But somehow, the five of us who had signed up managed to talk ourselves into it. The places would only go to waste if we didn't. Maybe we should do it as a last bit of training and help gain some much needed final swim training. Even Simon who had stuck rigidly to his training plan throughout, had become very adaptable and spontaneous.

'I am officially tapering at the moment,' he said. 'But what the hell? Let's do it.'

A company called Wild Running organised the Rocky Horror Swimrun event as part of a National Trust weekend of sporting events. It began at the beach at South Milton Sands and followed the South West Coast Path out to Salcombe and back. The course comprised four runs and four swims.

All five of us - Rachel, Ross, Simon, Kate and me - had been training for the RMIC, so were not too concerned about our fitness. The swimming and running were the least of our concerns. All of our worry was about what to wear. The unique aspect of swimrun events is that you must carry everything you need for the swims and the runs for the duration of the event. This means you either swim and run in the same clothes, or carry additional stuff with you in your tow float.

There is an entire industry based around dedicated swimrun equipment. Swimrun wetsuits are thinner, more breathable and flexible, allowing users to move seamlessly from water to land without the expected discomfort and chaffing of a full wetsuit. You can also get dedicated swimrun shoes, and others take measures such as drilling small holes into the soles of their expensive running shoes to allow water to drain quicker after exiting the water. Swimming in a pair of trainers is not recommended as they can be heavy and difficult to swim in. Hand paddles are allowed (sounds like cheating to me). As are pull buoys (a float that goes between your legs - definitely cheating). And fins or flippers can be used too (Pah! What next? A jetski?).

The thought of taking off our shoes and socks before each swim, trying to squash them into our tow floats, and then trying to clean sand and stones from our feet before putting our shoes and socks back on seemed too much of a faff. I also quite liked the novelty appeal of swimming in my trainers.

It brought back memories of the annual 'fun' life-saving session during school swimming lessons, when you would swim in your pyjamas and have to retrieve a rubber brick from the bottom of the pool. This was presumably supposed to prepare children for a scenario in life when you are out sleep-walking in your nightwear, and accidentally fall into some water but have to retrieve a rubber brick from the bottom before making it to shore. We've all been there.

Our local supermarket had rails of cheap shorty wetsuits for sale all summer, so I thought this could be a suitable solution. Unfortunately, the season had ended and there was one lone XXS wetsuit hidden on the 'seasonal' shelf at the back, which was now restocked with calculators, protractors and lunch boxes in anticipation of children returning to school. The five of us each scoured the local charity shops in search of shorty wetsuits but to no avail.

Instead, I opted to wear a pair of minimally padded lycra shorts that I wear for cycling and a rash vest. I could run and swim in this and also wear my barefoot shoes. Rachel went for a similar ensemble to me.

Kate wore a shorty wetsuit she borrowed from her daughter. Ross had a spare full-length wetsuit, which he cut the legs off with a pair of scissors, and Simon opted to wear a full length wetsuit for the entire run. Between us we looked like the biggest bunch of swimrun newbies it was possible to assemble.

The Rocky Horror Swimrun had a very civilised and unusual start time of 4.30pm, presumably to fit in with the high tide. Had the tide been low, the first swim would have been all on rock, making swimming a little trickier.

We soon established that there were just 11 of us signed up for the long swimrun. Our group of five made up almost half of the field (in case you struggle with maths).

There was also a swim only event taking place, so there were a dozen or so other swimmers gathered for the briefing at South Milton Sands. It was a very nice informal (chaotic) affair, with marshals not quite sure where we were going or what we were required to do. There wasn't too much that could go wrong, as we were simply keeping the sea on our right for the run (and on the left on the way back) and going for a few swims along the way.

Our group of five all compared our eclectic outfits and kit and we all seemed happy with our choices. As well as a whistle, we were also required to carry a tow float for safety, money, a mobile phone in a waterproof case, and a refillable cup or bottle to use at the aid stations. Other competitors had fancy collapsible cups. Rachel and I had an empty plastic bottle each that we squashed flat and tucked inside our tow floats.

Simon only realised as he was about to leave his house that he needed a cup, so grabbed a measuring cup from the kitchen drawer, pleased with how small and portable it was. It was so small it could hold just 70ml. While the rest of us would we sipping from our bottles and cups at the drinks stations, Simon would be downing shots.

The five of us agreed we would do the whole thing together. Kate is a much stronger swimmer than the rest of us, but wanted it to be a social event, so we all agreed to regather when back on dry land.

The dramatic and iconic arch of Thurlestone Rock, which is like a slightly smaller replica of Durdle Door, sits a little way off the beach at South Milton Sands. Our first swim was out and through this arch. From the beach, it didn't look too far or too intimidating, but then we found that the swim start/finish was much further down the eastern end of the beach, more than doubling the distance of the direct route.

The conditions were perfect and the sea was pleasantly calm, so we couldn't complain.

'I've got no idea what I'm doing, have you guys?' said a voice to our right.

We turned to see a man in full branded swimrun attire, complete with a pair of hand paddles, pull buoy, swim run shoes and a dedicated swimrun wetsuit.

'No, this is our first ever swimrun,' said Kate. 'We don't have a clue what we're doing. You look like you have all the gear.'

'All the gear, but no idea,' he said coyly.

'Is this your first swimrun?' asked Ross.

'Yes! Well... er... it's my first time doing this one. I've done a few others. I did a big one in the Brecon Beacons a couple of weeks ago.' And then he mumbled something about the national championships.

We wished him luck. He didn't sound like he needed it.

Within seconds of the swim start, Rachel, Simon, Ross and I were the four back markers. All the swim only competitors, Kate, and the rest of the Swimrun entrants, flailed off into the distance. Surprisingly for me, I quite enjoyed the swim. I didn't mind the sensation of swimming in my trainers. It felt like swimming in flippers. A pair of really shit flippers. And because Simon and Ross were both slightly slower swimmers than me, I didn't feel that I needed to swim too hard or fast. And compared to the prospect of the D-Day 6km swim a few weeks earlier, this was a doddle.

I tried to catch Rachel's eye, but when I did, there was a look of sheer panic across her face. She was breathing erratically and not looking like she was enjoying herself at all. There were plenty of kayakers and paddle boarders keeping an eye out for us, so there was never any concern for our safety. She looked like a different swimmer to the one who had found the D-Day swim so enjoyable.

We eventually reached Thurlestone Rock, passed through the arch, and began our return journey. There was no sign of Kate, but Rachel, Simon, Ross and I were all swimming fairly close together.

There had been regular jellyfish sightings along this stretch of coast in recent weeks, adding an additional level of fear. I spotted five or six during the swim, but they were all small and too far below me to pose any threat.

As we approached the beach, a swimmer powered past me. I found out after I was back on the beach that for the longer swim-only event, swimmers were to go out the arch and back twice. This guy had finished his two laps before we had completed one.

We made it back to shore after about 30 minutes. It was supposed to be half a mile, but my watch said 0.8 miles. It felt even longer than that. Kate had been on the beach for some time.

'Are you ok? How did you find that?' I asked Rachel.

'I really hated that. I find swimming in trainers so hard. It feels like I'm constantly fighting to stop myself sinking.'

'Yeah, it was a bit of a weird sensation, but I didn't mind it.'

Simon and Ross emerged from the water just behind us, both smiling, possibly with pleasure but more likely delight that the longest of our four swims was over. They both unpeeled the top half of their wetsuits and the five of us began the first of our run legs.

The stretch of coastline between South Milton Sands and Hope Cove is popular with walkers, as it's a fairly manageable gradient and there is ice cream and car parking at either end. It's a little over a mile up and over the headland and we passed couples, families and dog-walkers out enjoying the last days of summer. They all clapped and wished us luck, despite not knowing why we were running along the coast path with swimming hats and goggles on our heads.

As soon as we began running, Rachel seemed happier again.

'This is what my trainers are meant for,' she said. 'Running, not swimming!'

From Hope Cove, we swam from the beach at Outer Hope around the headland to Inner Hope. To our left, signs warned of unstable cliffs, and it felt we were swimming into No Hope. A couple of friendly support volunteers in kayaks guided us and offered words of encouragement.

This swim was supposed to be a quarter of a mile, but according to our watches was over half a mile. It felt even tougher than the first one, with currents pulling us in different directions, and the fatigue beginning to set in already. Our fourth and final swim would be identical to this one back at Hope Cove. This made it feel even tougher, knowing we had over 12 miles of running and another swim to contend with before we were back here.

We filled up our water bottles from a bowser and Simon necked a few shots with his measuring cup. Not only was his measuring cup impractically small, he had also secured it around his waist with a piece of string that was so short he could only get it to his mouth by performing an ambitious forward fold. It was hysterical to watch him try, but in the end we felt too sorry for him, so let him use our bottles instead.

This checkpoint also offered food. Big chunks of watermelon and Penguin chocolate bars. It's not a combination I had expected, but it was surprisingly good. After two swims in the sea, our tongues and lips were fizzing from the salt water and the watermelon was the perfect antidote.

The section between Hope Cove and North Sands in Salcombe is one of the toughest stretches of the South West Coast Path: 6.5 miles with 1,200 ft of climbing.

It was a stunning evening to be out running, though, and all five of us were very pleased we had decided to take part and not let our places go to waste. We were all taking it easy and enjoying the experience immensely.

As we ran along Bolberry Down, we were overtaken by a runner who was taking part in the short distance swimrun that began about half an hour after us.

'Is this the right way?' he asked.

'I've no idea. Sorry. We don't even really know where our route goes, let alone yours.'

'Oh well. It's a nice evening for it. Good luck, guys.'

And with that, he continued onward, refreshingly casual about whether or not he was going the right way.

We had been very pleased with the 4pm start. But the sun was low in the sky and we were still heading further away from the start. The course was an out and back and we would retrace our route along the coast path after our third swim in Salcombe. I looked at my watch and realised there was a very strong likelihood we would be running in the dark. A head torch was not on the kit list, as they assumed all competitors would be back before sunset. I don't think they had anticipated our level of amateurism.

Running along the coast path would be challenging in the dark with a light. It would be impossible and incredibly dangerous without. Rachel, Kate, Simon and Ross didn't seem too fazed by the lowering sun, so I didn't voice my concerns.

About two miles before we reached Salcombe, we met the guy who we had chatted to at the start in South Milton. The one who claimed to not know what he was doing. He was at least two miles and an entire swim ahead of us - so effectively an hour.

'Well done!' said Kate.

'I thought you had no idea what you were doing?' said Simon.

'Thanks guys. Well done, all of you.'

Then I called back and shouted over my shoulder, 'Hopefully you'll catch the person in front of you.'

He looked back at me, a little startled. I then became concerned that he might believe me and do himself some damage by chasing an imaginary race leader.

'Only joking!' I said. 'You are definitely in the lead.'

Ross's family and some other friends were there to cheer us on and hand out Jelly Babies at North Sands in Salcombe. The tide was fairly high and we waded out until the water came up to our waists and was deep enough to swim. Then we kept on wading, as it seemed preferable to swimming. It then rose up to our shoulders and we resorted to a moon-landing style bounce along the seabed. It was still preferable to swimming. One of the support kayakers laughed as we boinged past her. Eventually, when my head was disappearing fully underwater between bounces, I reluctantly began to swim.

This swim followed the rocky outcrop between the bays of North Sands and South Sands. In my head, and on a map, it should have been a very short and easy swim. But a combination of currents, tiredness, a pair of trainers, and a general crapness at swimming made it very slow going. We were hugging close to the rocks and we seemed to make very little progress forwards.

The sea was dark and eerie in this section, which made me want to get it over and done with as quickly as possible. Rachel had resorted to leisurely breaststroke, but was still quicker than my frantic front crawl.

When we eventually made it round to South Sands, we did the same as we had at the start of the swim and put our feet down at the earliest opportunity and bounced our way into shore.

'I'm in awe of you guys,' said the marshal at the checkpoint.

'We are in awe of you. Thank you for giving up your time to look after weirdos like us.'

There were just 11 of us taking part in the long swimrun and, taking into account those manning the drinks stations and the water safety support, there must have been over 20 marshals. We felt very honoured and grateful for these wonderful volunteers. It made us even more glad we had decided to take part. The event would have felt very quiet if we hadn't turned up. We were the last five to pass through the checkpoint, and we hoped we had not held them up too long.

It was a slow trudge back up to the coast path from South Sands, past the National Trust owned Overbecks, around the dramatic Sharp Tor, past Starehole Bay and back towards Hope Cove. We reached the extremely steep valley at Soar Mill Cove, which is a steep climb down and then an equally steep climb up. I had brought two packets of salt and vinegar Hula Hoops with me, stashed in my tow float.

It was time to bring them out.

'Who wants some Hula Hoops?' I said.

'No need, fella,' said Simon proudly. 'I've brought my own packet this time.'

He reached into a pocket in the back of his rash vest and pulled out a packet.

'Ah, shit. I think my packet has split,' he said.

'Oh no. Have they got wet?'

'Er... yeah.'

Not only were Simon's Hula Hoops wet, but because the packet had been crushed under his tight wetsuit while swimming and running for three hours, they had turned into a mushy puree. As he gently squeezed the packet, the contents oozed from a hole in one of the corners in a paste. 'I supposed it might still be edible,' he said, squirting a bit into his mouth.

'How does it taste?' I asked.

'Fucking revolting,' he said, spitting it into the gorse. 'It turns out crisps don't taste great after soaking in seawater for three hours.'

'Thanks for the advice. I'll try to remember that. It's a good job I brought two,' I said, handing Simon a dry packet.

'You're a legend. Thank you.'

The sun was setting and we were still over a mile from Hope Cove, which is where we would do our fourth and final swim.

'Do you think they will allow us to swim if it's dark?' I said.

'I'm not sure,' said Ross. 'I don't think they mentioned any cutoff times anywhere.'

'No, but I don't think they expected it to take us this long,' said Rachel.

'What do we do if they don't let us swim?' asked Kate.

'I don't think I would be too bothered,' I said. 'Would you?'

'No. I think I'd probably be secretly delighted.'

It wasn't so much the swim that I was concerned about, as there would probably still be enough twilight for us to at least find our way around the headland. What worried me most was running the last stretch of coast path to the finish at South Milton Sands when it would be pitch black.

'I don't think we should worry,' said Simon. 'If they allow us to do the swim, we should do it. If they don't then we don't.'

'Sounds like a plan.'

As we crested the hill after Bolberry Down before descending to Hope Cove, a familiar figure emerged from the half-light. It was Ceri, the race director.

'Hey guys! How are you all doing?' he said.

'Pretty good thanks.'

'Are all five of you together?'

'Yes. I think we are the final five.'

He looked mightily relieved. He had set out to look for five of his race competitors, who were still out on the course after sunset. It would have been mildly concerning if we were spread out over the remote stretch of coastline in the dark.

'Yes, sorry to keep you waiting,' said Simon.

'Oh, not at all. I'm just glad you are all ok. I'm afraid that I have some disappointing news. As it is now so dark, you will not be able to do the final swim in Hope Cove. It just isn't safe. But you'll still be able to continue the run all the way to the finish. Is that ok?'

There were no protests from any of us. We didn't want to act as though we were pleased to be told we couldn't complete the final swim, but we were all secretly fist pumping inside. We thanked Ceri for putting on such a fun event and descended the long hill into Hope Cove.

'Do you think they will mark us down as DNF?' said Rachel.

'I don't know,' I said. 'I guess so. Although we would have done the swim if we had been allowed. It's not our fault the start time was so close to sunset.'

By the time we reached Hope Cove, we knew they had made the correct call by not allowing us to swim. The last mile between Hope Cove and South Milton was a little tricky in the faded light and would have been incredibly dangerous 20 minutes later.

We staggered onto the pitch black beach at South Milton Sands, where we began our race nearly five hours earlier. We were the final five of the eleven starters to cross the line. They gave us all the same finishing time so we technically finished joint 7th (which sounds much better than joint last), and they kindly didn't mark us down as DNF, which was an added bonus.

It had been a really enjoyable few hours and a unique way to spend time with friends. We had all survived unscathed and had hopefully benefited from some last-minute swim training for the RMIC. Swimming in a wetsuit and without a pair of trainers should feel easy in comparison.

TWELVE

Things didn't go quite to plan in the weeks leading up to the Royal Marines Iron Challenge. I strained my hip while crossing a road, which was one of the most bizarre injuries I have ever had. I was walking across and saw a car approaching, so moved from a slow walk to a light jog, tweaking something in my hip during the process. It was very painful for a few days, and I wondered whether it was going to impact the RMIC. Fortunately it seemed to disappear as quickly as it arrived.

Then I twisted my knee painfully at a water park. It was one of those big inflatable obstacle courses in a lake and we had gone there at the end of the school holidays, two weeks before the RMIC. The lifeguard blew her whistle to signify the end of our session while I was standing on top of a large inflatable cube, about 10ft above the water. I jumped from the top into the water below, trying to end the session in style with a bomb to impress my kids. But I didn't tuck my legs up tightly enough, and as I hit the water, my left leg twisted awkwardly out and I felt an agonising pain on the inside of my left knee. I kept quiet about it at the time, because I didn't want to admit I had injured myself doing a bomb off an inflatable water obstacle, but it felt like I had done something quite serious.

Almost a year later, that left knee is still not right. Whenever I play football, or twist it slightly, I feel the familiar pain. But thankfully, I soon realised that providing my knee joint moves in a straight direction - swimming, cycling and running - then it doesn't cause any problems.

Then, in the week before the RMIC, I developed an issue with my ears. They felt like they were permanently blocked with water, or wax, or both. On the couple of occasions I went swimming, I found it difficult to stand up when I got out of the water, and it took a long time for me to regain my balance.

I bought some ear drops about three days before the event, hoping it would be sorted in time. There was a slightly unnerving, fizzing sensation when I applied the drops, which I hoped meant it was doing its thing. Later that evening, there was no improvement. I tried them twice the next day and then the evening before the RMIC, and the fizzing continued, and now my ears seemed more blocked than they had before. My hearing was extremely muffled and my balance felt off even just walking around the house. The thought of swimming 2.4 miles, cycling 112 miles and then running a marathon seemed impossible.

If any of these ailments - the strained hip, twisted knee, or blocked ear - had happened to Rachel, I would have put it down as a classic case of maranoia (pre-race paranoia). I would have told her, subtly, that she was being a hypochondriac and that it would be absolutely fine. But it's only maranoia when it's an ailment of someone else. When it's something happening to me, it is very real indeed.

Rachel is usually struck down with maranoia before every event. Strangely for this one, she was relatively injury and illness free.

Her problems instead lay with her bike.

It was looking like she might not even have a bike for the event. She had booked hers in for a service two weeks before and they told her it would be ready in a couple of days. They then diagnosed various issues with the rear cassette and the derailleur and some other bits whose function is a mystery to me. Rachel allowed them to proceed, but they had difficulty ordering the parts in time. Rachel made a few contingency plans, and I even offered to let her use my bike and I could borrow my dad's old one that I had borrowed for my last Ironman (I'd done one before, remember? I don't like to talk about it much). There was even talk of bringing The Falcon out of retirement (see Free Country: A Penniless Adventure the Length of Britain).

Thankfully, two days before the event, Rachel's bike was fixed. She was ready. She believed she was capable.

There had been various equipment discussions in the group chat in the months building up to the RMIC, as people compared tri-suits, cycling shoes, bikes, wetsuits and goggles. Lots had bought new expensive goggles with fancy polarizing lenses. Rachel bought me a pair for my birthday, but I asked her to return them as I planned to stick with my old faithfuls that I had been wearing for the last six years. They were scratched and leaked occasionally, but seemed to do the job.

In the week before the event, panic broke out about the dark lenses of everyone else's goggles. It was not until a few weeks before the event that we realised we would be beginning our swim at 05.30am - nearly one and a half hours before sunrise. It would be pitch black and those with the fancy goggles were worried about not being able to see a thing.

Anyone else panic buying clear goggles? wrote Tim.

Another group member then tried wearing his fancy goggles in the bath with the lights off. It turns out he couldn't see anything. Another set an alarm for the same time that our swim would be and stood in the garden in his pants and a pair of goggles. They couldn't see much either. Just to wind everyone up, I posted a photo I found on google images of some tropical fish on a coral reef. I told them I took the photo during a swim at midnight in the local estuary through the lenses of my old goggles. Most of the group ended up buying cheap pairs of clear goggles days before the event. I felt annoyingly smug with my old faithfuls.

I always sleep really badly the night before a big event. The pre-race nerves kick in and I feel anxious about all the preparation. I'm mostly just anxious about getting some sleep before my alarm sounds at a stupid time in the morning. Ours was set for 3am.

All of our stuff - bikes, wetsuits, food, running kit - was packed in the van for our early start. We only needed to get up, get dressed, have a cup of tea and drive to the race start. We had even pre-made some breakfast peanut butter bagels.

Over optimistically, Rachel and I went to bed at 7pm, hoping to get a full eight hours sleep. We were still lying awake at 11pm but thankfully dozed off soon after, for four very restless hours. I have always accepted that I sleep badly the night before. Rachel told me she heard or read somewhere that it's the night before the night before that is the most important. I've no idea if this is true, but I tend to hold this as a fact. The night before the night before, I had a brilliant night's sleep, so I had no excuses.

There were fewer than 100 people taking part in the RMIC, but the race directors had gone to a lot of trouble with the organisation. Race HQ looked fantastic as we pulled into the car park at 3.30am on the morning of the event. There was an enormous *Finish* arch illuminated with spotlights, music blaring out of some big speakers, and several stalls set up from local sponsors.

'Are you taking part or just here to support?' said the smiliest marshal I have ever seen.

'We are taking part unfortunately,' I said.

'Fantastic. I'm so impressed. I am sure you'll have an amazing day. It will all be worth it. Just turn left after the barrier here and my husband will direct you where to park.'

'Thank you.'

The following morning, we got chatting to this smiling lady when we came back to Blackpool Sands for a post-event breakfast. She and her husband had been down in Devon on holiday for a week's camping. They had packed up and were heading home, and called into Blackpool Sands to have some lunch before their journey. As they sat and ate, they watched people assembling gazebos, erecting barrier fencing and inflating the finishing arch. They asked what was going on and one of the race directors told them all about the Royal Marines Iron Challenge. They were so excited about the event that they asked if there was anything they could do to help. An hour later that had re-erected their tent in the car park field, and were marshaling the car park from 3am the next morning. When we told them how amazing we thought they were, they acted like they were the ones who had been given a gift.

Six years previously, back in Vichy, France, when I was preparing all of my stuff in the bike transition area, it was a daunting and lonely experience. I knew nobody, barely spoke the language, and had no idea of what I was in store for. It was also quite an impersonal experience as Ironman is such a big, anonymous brand.

It was very different at the RMIC. Of the 20 people getting their stuff ready in the transition area at the same time as Rachel and me, we knew half of them. This time I spoke the language. And this time I had some idea of what was in store. We now knew all three race directors pretty well, and they were walking about chatting to those taking part. It sounds cliched to say, but it did feel like a big RMIC family.

It was very reassuring to be surrounded by familiar faces. We all compared our lack of sleep, nervousness, and the number of toilet visits we'd had so far that morning.

The sea was pancake flat, there was not a breath of wind, and it was forecast to stay dry for the rest of the day. The thought of swimming 2.4 miles in the sea was terrifying. Swimming most of it in the dark felt deeply traumatic. But the prospect of doing it all in the dark during horrendous conditions had filled us all with dread for weeks.

There was a lot of hanging around before the race start. Being the first time the event had taken place, the organisers wanted to ensure they had enough time to do the briefing and issue the tow floats and GPS trackers.

Each swimmer was given two glow sticks, the kind that you might find at a 90s rave. One was to be attached to the zip on the back of our wetsuit, the other to our tow float. Inside the tow float was a GPS tracker. We had to take this from the tow float after the swim and keep it with us during the bike and run, to provide live coverage of where we were on the course, so that organisers (and friends and family) could keep an eye on us.

My ears felt horrendous on the morning of the event. I decided the best course of action was to protect them as much as possible to eliminate the possibility of them getting worse and ending my race before I had even finished the swim. I had never swum in ear plugs before, so didn't want to try that for the first time during the event. The swim hats were tight fitting, so I pulled it down snugly over my ears and hoped that would be enough.

As we stood by the waterside, they gave us one final briefing. I couldn't hear anything because of my blocked ears and swim hat, so I temporarily rolled up the latex on both sides of my head.

The swim comprised three laps of a giant triangle of Blackpool Sands bay. Each lap was about 1,300 metres. That's 52 lengths of a standard swimming pool.

'Just head towards the flashing red buoy in the distance,' said the race director.

'What buoy?' I whispered to Rachel.

'I think that's it over there.'

I lifted my goggles and still couldn't see anything.

'I can't see any flashing buoy. Oh well, it's not as if I'm going to be leading. I'll just follow everyone else.'

As we all wandered down to the water's edge at 5.25am for the start of the race, I didn't feel the level of fear I had expected to. Wading out into the treacle-black sea, surrounded by glow sticks, was one of the most surreal moments of my life, and it genuinely felt like some sort of out-of-body experience. It seemed so bizarre, so utterly stupid, to be attempting to swim 2.4 miles in the sea IN THE DARK, that I had gone way beyond fear. If I had thought too much about what we were actually about to undertake, I would have either broken down in tears or turned and run straight back up the beach. Instead, I just slipped into this weird, trance-like state of acceptance.

Rachel seemed remarkably calm too, considering what she was about to undertake.

'Good luck!' I said, giving her a big hug. 'Try to enjoy it.'

'I will try,' she said, taking a deep breath. 'You too.'

We wished good luck to those around us. In the dark, and all wearing identical outfits, it was impossible to tell who was who. We all swam out towards the starter buoy, there was a countdown, and then we were off. I put my face in the water and received an accidental kick in the face from the swimmer in front of me. I came up for air and saw Rachel already a couple of strokes ahead. I realised I might not see her again until the end of the race.

As with every swim event I have ever done (except the Rocky Horror Swimrun), the erratic breathing set in straight away. I then felt like I was being overtaken by everyone, so tried to up my speed, which exacerbated the problem and made my breathing even more laboured. After a few minutes, I managed to get it more under control. But something seemed different. And it wasn't the fact I was swimming without my trainers.

It was another ten minutes before I realised what it was. After I had rolled my swim hat up on the beach to listen to the briefing, I had forgotten to roll it back down. Sea water was swooshing in and out of both ears constantly, causing an extremely bizarre audio sensation. I considered treading water and readjusting it, but knew my goggle straps were now in the way and that all I would do was trap more water in my ears. I decided to try to ignore it instead.

The swimmers soon spread out and I still couldn't see the red flashing light we were heading towards, so instead just followed the glow sticks of the swimmers in front of me and hoped they could see where they were going.

Looking ahead, the other swimmers were like glowworms. Looking back over my shoulder, I could see nothing and assumed I must be last. Oh well, I was fairly close to the people in front, so it didn't worry me too much.

I eventually caught sight of the flashing buoy and it still looked much further away than I expected. Over to my right, I could see some green dots which must be swimmers already on the second side of the triangle.

It felt like I had been in the water for a very long time, but when I checked my watch as I rounded the first buoy, it showed I had only been swimming for eight minutes.

The second side of the triangle was significantly longer than the first and third. Over to my right, I could now see a few glow sticks of swimmers who were behind me and still on the first section. Because of the sticks being tied to our backs and tow floats, other swimmers were not visible when looking behind. When I spoke to others after the event, apparently everyone thought they were last during that first section of the swim.

I finished the first lap in about 31 minutes, which I knew wasn't a sustainable speed, but it allowed me plenty of time to get round the remaining two laps inside the cutoff. The sky was beginning to lighten for the second lap, and the swim became a lot more enjoyable. I could now make out dark, eerie shapes under the water as we swam. Close to the first buoy, I saw what I thought could be a seal or even a barrel jelly fish, which made me quicken my stroke. On the third lap, I discovered it was just a rock.

Midway through the first lap, I had seen a swimmer to my left that looked a bit like Rachel. She had the same wetsuit as Rachel (as did most of us) and the same swimming style (again, fairly similar to everyone's). As we began the third and final lap, she was still there. Now the sky was brighter, I realised it was Rachel. I swam breaststroke for a while and eventually got her attention.

'Hello, fancy seeing you here!' she said.

'How are you doing?'

'I love it! Isn't it amazing? It's so beautiful.'

'Er... yeah. I wouldn't say I'm loving it. I'm looking forward to it all being over. I'm finding it really hard.'

'I'm having a brilliant time.'

A few days later, we watched a digital video of our trackers during the race (sped up, obviously. We wouldn't watch it in real time), and Rachel and I were next to each other the entire time. Yet it wasn't until the start of the third lap that we realised.

I heard from my mum later that night that they had been up early, following the online tracker. Rachel and I had been swimming closely together, and then my tracker just stopped. Rachel swam off and left me and I was stranded in the middle of the ocean. They were a little concerned that I had drowned. Not as concerned as mum had been about Roger during the East Devon Round. And not concerned enough to actually do anything about it, but concerned enough to send me a text which I didn't get until much later saying, *I hope you haven't drowned. *winky face*.*

As I staggered up the beach, I experienced a different sensation to my recent swims. My legs felt wobbly and my arms and shoulders ached, as you would expect after a 2.4 mile sea swim. But the extreme dizziness and imbalance I had felt on recent swims, and even while walking around the house, had gone. Everything sounded louder - the crowd cheering, the crunch of the pebbles beneath my feet, the lapping of the waves on the shore. I could hear! My ears were finally unblocked! It was a miracle! I was cured!

If you're suffering with blocked ears, try an extreme irrigation technique of a 1 hour 40 minute sea swim without a hat over your ears. It worked a treat for me.

The euphoria I experienced after finishing my Ironman swim six years earlier came flooding back to me. It's such a bizarre feeling. Never would you expect to be excited about the prospect of cycling 112 miles, followed by a full marathon. But the satisfaction of being back on dry land after such a physically strenuous and mentally challenging swim makes anything but being in the water seem exciting.

Rachel and I exited the water at exactly the same time. And only a few seconds further up the beach was our friend Tim. We peeled off our wetsuits and began to get changed next to our bikes. The changing tent had looked a little crowded that morning, so we just left our transition box by our bikes and stripped off in the open air instead.

I put on my helmet just as Rachel did the same. Tim grabbed his bike and then fumbled with his helmet and sent his bike crashing to the floor. He picked it up and the three of us jogged slowly to the start line to begin the first of four 28-mile loops.

There can't be many tougher starts to a triathlon bike leg than the RMIC. The beach at Blackpool Sands is nestled in a valley on the south Devon coast, and the road climbs from the car park for 2km up to the village of Strete. Two weeks earlier, the Tour of Britain (the less famous cousin of the Tour de France) passed through here. The hill from Blackpool Sands was classified as a Category Two climb and was one of three King of the Mountains climbs on the 190km stage.

Not only was this hill the very first thing we had to navigate after clipping into our pedals, but we were going to have to cycle up it four times.

It was a hill we were very familiar with having cycled it regularly in the buildup to the RMIC. In fact, this hill was part of Rachel's first ever triathlon, way back in 2016 (see DNF 1), where she crashed into a hedge cycling around an uphill bend.

The steepest section comes at the start, but you are rewarded with stunning views of the beach at Blackpool Sands below to the left. We could just make out the green hats of the last remaining swimmers in the water. It was surreal to think we had just swum three big laps of the bay.

Tim, Rachel and I cycled up the first hill together. We were chatting and joking and were soon at the summit in Strete without really realising it.

A long, fast descent followed down to the start of the Slapton Line, the long, straight barrier spit with the freshwater of Slapton Ley on one side, and the sea on the other.

There was a slight prevailing south-westerly wind forecast for most of the day, which meant a headwind on each of the four times we cycled the Slapton Line. Compared to how conditions could have been, we had no complaints. It was 7.30am on a Sunday morning and the roads were pretty much empty.

Tim is much faster along the flat than me and within a few seconds, he was up the road ahead. At some point along the Slapton Line, I looked back and Rachel had dropped back slightly. I knew she wouldn't want me to wait for her, and drafting was against the rules, so I continued on at my own speed.

A tremendous benefit of the Tour of Britain passing through here a couple of weeks earlier was that the local council filled in all the potholes along this section. Only about a third of our 28 mile loop was on the Tour of Britain's route, so the rest was still littered with Devon's infamous potholes, but for this section, at least, we got to enjoy some immaculately surfaced roads.

There's a long steady climb from Torcross to the village of Stokenham, and as I reached the top, I caught up with Tim again.

'Only five of my bloody gears are working!' he said.

'Really? Didn't you just have your bike serviced?'

'Yes, I'm so annoyed. I'm going to give the bike shop a call tomorrow. It's SO annoying.'

I have had my fair share of event mishaps. During my first Ironman, I lost my timing chip minutes before the start of the race, only to discover it was stuck to the velcro on my wetsuit. Just before we were called into the water for the Cotswold 113, I realised my tri-suit was on back-to-front, and had to strip naked to correct my mistake. But Tim's bad luck is legendary. There is some sort of calamity that befalls him each time we go out. We have run several DIY marathons together, and on each one he has either stopped his watch too early, or forgot to unpause it midway round, or there's been some GPS glitch, so he has recorded a series of almost marathons. We'll be heading out for a bike ride and he will always have a bike malfunction before setting off.

The night before the RMIC, Tim sent a message out on the group chat asking if anyone had a spare hydration bladder, because his had somehow sprung a leak. Then, his bike managed to get a flat tyre sitting in his van. Having only five gears to cycle 112 hilly miles was not good news for Tim. Hopefully, it would mean I stood a better chance of keeping up with him, though.

Rachel's mum and dad were down in Devon on holiday and came out to watch us on the bike leg. I passed them at the roadside about 10 miles into the loop.

'Oh, it's you,' they shouted. 'Well done, George.'

'Thank you! Rachel shouldn't be too far behind.'

'We know. She's due here any second. We are following her on the tracker. Good luck!

I then saw Ruth, a friend of ours, standing on the pavement a little further up the road.

'Go on, Rachel!' she said.

I looked back over my shoulder, assuming Rachel must have caught me up, but there was nobody there.

'Go on, Rachel!' shouted Ruth again. 'Oh, you're not Rachel. Hi George!'

'Hi Ruth,' I said, a little perplexed.

I then passed another friend who shouted 'well done, Rachel!' at me. Again, I looked over my shoulder, but there was no sign of her. I was beginning to get a complex. Why did everyone think I was Rachel? And why was everyone cheering for her and not me?

At the top of each hill, Tim pushed on and then I caught him again on the next uphill section. Had it not been for his gearing issue, I probably wouldn't have seen him at all.

We caught up with Kate, the fastest swimmer in our group of 11. She was grinning from ear to ear. There's some weird sensation that descends upon you during an event like this. For months you've been fretting about it. For months, it occupies much of your mental energy, mostly in an anxious way. And then the day suddenly arrives and you're in the middle of it. It's no longer this terrifying thing off in the distance. It's something that's happening. It's something that you're doing.

And maybe it's not so bad after all. I mean, obviously it's very tough, and is only going to get tougher, but you're here. And you're taking part.

That was written on Kate's face and almost all the other competitors we saw on those first couple of bike laps.

Things didn't stay so positive for long.

There were two feed stations on the bike loop. One at Strete Gate, a couple of miles from the start, and the other halfway round. I had food in my back pocket and two full water bottles, so aimed to keep going until I reached the halfway station on the second lap.

People were still shouting out for Rachel. It was becoming very disconcerting. All the friends I passed at the roadside seemed disappointed to see me. They were only interested in Rachel.

One of the snacks I had brought with me that I was trying for the first time was roast potatoes. Obviously I've tried roast potatoes before - I'm a massive fan. But I've never carried them with me to eat during an event. I had heard good things from a few people, so thought I would give them a go.

I cut the potatoes quite small and roasted them with lots of salt, and a couple of vegetable stock pots to give them some extra flavour. They were brown, crispy and looked incredible, so I brought two zip-lock bags full. One tucked into the back pocket of my cycling jersey, the other in my backpack, ready for the run.

About 20 miles into the bike ride, I decided to have my first potato. I reached into my back pocket and slid one out of the bag while cycling. I popped it into my mouth. I regretted it instantly. It was the saltiest thing I had ever tasted. All the moisture inside my mouth evaporated. The two stock pots plus the all the added salt was a bad idea. I then remembered I had sprinkled some extra salt on them after they had cooked, just to make sure they were salty enough. They were definitely salty enough. It took me ten minutes, and most of my water, to swallow that first potato. Salt is apparently good for preventing cramping. It is unlikely I will ever cramp again after eating that potato.

Strangely, after I eventually swallowed it, I almost wanted another. It was so strong, so intense, that it also took my mind off the cycling for a few minutes.

'Well done, Rachel!' shouted another person as I passed through the village of Stoke Fleming. They did a double-take and looked a little confused. But not as confused as me.

I caught and passed Tim on the hill out of Blackpool Sands at the start of the second lap. He was still raging about his five gears. He had distracted himself from the cycling by rehearsing the verbal battering he was going to give to the bike shop who serviced his bike. I didn't want to be in their shoes.

Watching video footage from one of the race directors a couple of days later, it reminded Tim how he had dropped his bike during the first transition, landing it heavily on the rear-derailleur. It was at this point he realised why he only had five gears. Thankfully, he had not yet got round to phoning the bike shop.

Tim flew past me on the Slapton Line again, and then stopped when he reached Torcross, where his family had parked up in the car park to give him food and refill his water bottles.

Midway through the second lap, I saw my mum's car parked up in a layby. There, stood beyond the car, were my mum, dad and Layla. After years of not attending any events, my mum and dad had now been to two in two months. And this time, they had come on purpose, rather than by coincidence on their way back from Lidl. Leo and Kitty had gone off to friends' houses, and Layla had stayed at home on her own. My mum and dad had picked her up, insistent that she would want to come and cheer us on. Layla was standing there eating a massive bag of Doritos, looking totally disinterested.

'Oh, you're not Rachel,' said my mum.

'Why does everyone keep saying that?' I said as I pulled into the layby and unclipped.

'Because you are down on the tracker as Rachel. We thought you had drowned. Your tracker was stopped in the middle of the sea for ages. It's moving again now. It's about a mile behind you. Presumably you and Rachel have accidentally got each other's trackers.'

'Ah, that explains a lot. People have been calling me Rachel since the start.'

Still, it was nice to know that even when my mum thought I was drowned at sea, she still came out to cheer on Rachel on the bike leg.

'Well done, Dord,' said my dad. 'How's it going?'

'Yeah, not too bad thanks. I'm getting a bit bored with cycling. And there's still about 70 miles to go.'

'Just keep going. You're doing really well.'

'Thanks for coming out to see us, Layla. It's great to see you.'

'I didn't have much choice,' she said.

'Are you having fun?'

'Wonderful.'

'Lovely to see you all. I won't be passing here again for another two hours so don't hang around.'

'Don't worry, we won't,' said Layla.

I called into the feed station a couple of miles later. It was manned by a team of young cadets and they set to work like a Formula One pit stop crew.

'What can we get you?' said one, as I unclipped.

Another grabbed hold of my bike and stood there with it.

'We've got ginger cake, crisps, brownies, flapjack, jelly babies, coke, water,' said another.

'Er... that sounds amazing. I'm just going to use the toilet first.'

'Shall we fill your water bottles with water while you go?'

'Wow, yes please. That would be great.'

I went to the toilet then wolfed down a handful of crisps, stuffed a flapjack into my mouth, said thanks to the cadets, and rejoined the route.

I had brought a few electrolyte tablets that I forgot to add to my water at the feed station. I then stupidly tried to put one into my water bottle while cycling along. I spilled water over my hands opening the bottle, then with my hands soaking wet, I tried to retrieve a tablet from the ziplock bag in my pocket. The tablets began fizzing in the bag, so I carried around a bag of foam for the next 70 miles.

In the weeks before the RMIC, the local council had been doing some roadworks outside Dartmouth. They filtered traffic down to one lane and there were temporary traffic lights in place. If you got caught here at the wrong time, you could be held up by about five minutes. Get this bad luck each time on the four-lap bike leg, and that's a 20 minute delay. That could be the difference between making the cutoff and not.

The organisers were understandably anxious about this and put in several calls to the local council. By the morning of the RMIC, the road workers had packed up and left.

They then tried to close another stretch of road on the route early in the morning on race day. It happened to be directly outside the house where one of the competitors lived. Their wife went outside and had a very polite word with them and persuaded them to take the rest of the day off and come back tomorrow.

It is an especially hilly loop. There's about 2,300 feet of climbing in a 28 mile loop, which means over 9,000 feet for the full bike leg. To put this into perspective, my previous Ironman in Vichy, France, had what they described as a 'hilly' bike leg, and its total elevation was a little under 4,000 feet. They have since changed the bike course in Vichy and made it a little more challenging, but it is still a long way off that of the RMIC.

I was feeling pretty good and enjoying the bike leg much more than I thought I would. Compared to my cycle round Dartmoor in the blistering August sun with the face mask round my chin, this was very enjoyable.

I even quite liked the hills. Cycling on the flat is my weakness. My lower back gets very uncomfortable and I spend most of the time sitting up like a French man out for his morning croissants. The hills are a chance to change the rhythm, stand up on the pedals, give my back a bit of a stretch.

I felt strong cycling up the hills, though. Mostly because I was comparing myself to five-gear-Tim, who was understandably not enjoying the hills so much.

Lap three of the four was the toughest. On lap one I was still on a high from surviving the swim, lap two I was still feeling quite fresh. Lap three, however, felt much more difficult. There was the knowing feeling that we would cycle over this exact same ground again in another two hours' time.

Before I knew it, I was onto Blackpool Sands hill for the fourth and final time. This time felt so much better. This time I knew that every inch I cycled of this lap would be the last. Every inch was getting closer to the finish.

It's a strange set of emotions that pass through you during an event like this. You can be high on life one minute, and then feeling at your absolute lowest only seconds later. You can be laughing with a fellow competitor one minute and then crying about something trivial the next.

At the top of the hill, just before the village of Strete, I passed two vintage buses parked at the side of the road. Several men in high viz vests were loitering at the front of one bus, looking flustered. Both buses were full of fairly gloomy looking passengers.

There was water gushing all over the road, which was coming from a big dent in the front radiator grill of one of the buses. A dent in the rear of the other bus suggested one had crashed into the other.

These buses take part in a special vintage bus day every year. Many of the usual bus routes out of Dartmouth were replaced with these vintage buses for the day.

At the top of that hill, almost 85 miles into a bike ride, I felt tearful for this bus driver. They would have spent months preparing for this day, getting the buses ready, making sure they were all running well and looking their absolute best. And then the excitement of the actual day, showing off these beautiful classic vehicles to members of the public. The excited couples and families, many perhaps on holiday, enjoying a day out along the Devon coast in a vintage bus. And then one driver ends up smacking into the back of another.

It was all I could think about for the next few miles. My day was glorious compared to his.

I passed and overtook Tim on the hill and he flew past me again on the Slapton Line.

'You might only have five gears, but they are five bloody good gears,' I shouted.

Midway through lap four, I passed John. John was one of the eleven from our local group. He is a strong swimmer but cycling and running were fairly new to him. He had put in a lot of preparation and trained hard.

'Hey John. How are you doing?' I asked.

'Oh, hi George. Yeah, good thanks. Just having something to eat. How are you doing?'

'Not too bad, thanks. Looking forward to getting off my bike.'

'Me too. Have a good one.'

It was a few minutes later that I started to question myself. Although he sounded really positive, it was clear by the speed he was travelling that John had been struggling. I felt bad that I did not stay with him for longer to make sure he was ok and to offer some words of encouragement. It was the selfish part of me that had kicked in. I was finding it extremely tough too, and I just wanted to finish. I was so close to the end now and I didn't want to delay it any longer. But I should have stayed with him for a bit. I should have helped.

I caught Tim again and apparently he had cycled straight past John too. I felt a little better. At least I wasn't the only selfish asshole.

Tim and I cycled the final few miles together. The ride finishes with a long, fast, and quite scary descent down to Blackpool Sands.

Swim done.

Bike done.

Now just the small matter of a hilly trail marathon.

I had opted for a complete change of clothes for the run. I was trying to get changed discreetly in the open air transition area when one of the race directors stuck a GoPro in my face as I was midway through taking my cycling shorts off and began asking me how I found the bike leg, and what were my feelings about my run.

I gave a polite (and very brief) answer, as I awkwardly tried to get dressed without giving him a full frontal flash for his race movie.

'How are you feeling? Did you enjoy the cycle?'

'Errr... I think enjoy is a strong word. I'm glad it's over. Now just a marathon to go. It's very flat, isn't it?'

He laughed. 'Oh, absolutely. It's pancake flat the whole way.'

He eventually moved on to interview another competitor, and I finished getting dressed.

One of our friends who was there to spectate told us that Rachel was about half an hour behind us. She was cycling just behind Kate (although Rachel later said she hadn't even known Kate was just ahead). To any friends and family tracking us from home, however, I would have been cycling with Kate all morning, and Rachel with Tim. All sorts of rumours would be circulating.

Tim and I left the transition at the same time. Having been on several runs and bike rides together in the build-up to the event, it was a fitting coincidence that after 1.5 hours in the water and nearly eight hours on the bike, we were beginning the run at the exact same time.

We later watched the video of our friend Martin, who arrived back at transition minutes before the cutoff. Rather than the leisurely transition Tim and I had - changing into a whole new outfit, taking the time to eat some food and make sure we had everything we needed - Martin had to dump his bike and run. He ran, panting and swearing to begin his run, while still wearing his cycling gloves and helmet. The rear pocket of his cycling jersey was still stuffed full of supplies from the cycling leg and it bounced up and down as he ran, like a pair of bollocks hanging from his back. It was very amusing to watch.

The road we had followed for the bike leg hugs the coast and takes some of the sting out of the gradient. The South West Coast Path, however, which we would be running, goes straight up the steepest part of the hill. It is impossible to run up and a considerable effort to walk.

It was a good time to eat and give the different muscles in our legs a chance to wake up. I cracked open the first of many bags of Hula Hoops. I had a backpack full of snacks:

sandwiches, cold pizza, crisps, flapjack, oh and some inedible salty roast potatoes.

I had meant to tell the race directors about the mix-up with mine and Rachel's trackers. I figured they would need to know, just in case it messed up the race results. I didn't want to cross the line later and be handed a trophy for the first female or something. As we trudged up the hill, I phoned one of the race directors and explained the situation. They said they would amend the details on their tracking system.

While I was on the phone, Tim and I unknowingly walked straight past the stile out of the field and continued up to the top corner where there was no exit. If it wasn't for a call from someone further back down the hill, we would have continued in the wrong direction for longer.

This call came from John, the friend Tim and I had abandoned in his time of need. And now here he was, saving our bacon. Tim and I thanked him for getting us back on track. John told us how he had been in a bad way when we had seen him on the bike. Not long after I passed him, some kind former Royal Marine had cycled past and chatted to him, and rather than selfishly cycling off and leaving him, he had stuck with John until the end. That's what Marines do. No man left behind. Tim and I felt even guiltier.

At the top of the hill there was a big field of cows and the coast path cut straight across. On previous runs, Rachel and I had sensibly followed the perimeter of the field instead and given the cows a wide berth. With no desire to run a metre further than absolutely necessary, this time we ran straight through the middle of them all.

After passing through the cow field, the path crosses the main road and then descends steeply into the valley that funnels down to the beautiful Landcombe Cove - a beach that I regularly catch glimpses of when running or cycling but have never visited. The path ascends the other side, passes through the village of Strete and then descends via a series of steep switchbacks through the woods to the beach at Strete Gate.

'That's the hardest bit done,' said Tim, forgetting we were going to have to do all of it again at the very end of the marathon. 'I reckon if we push on a bit we can do a sub five-hour marathon.'

'Sub five hours? I think that's very unlikely,' I said.

'I feel ok at the moment. How about you?'

'Yeah, I feel ok, too. But we've swum 2.4 miles and cycled 112 miles. I don't think we'll be feeling great for long.'

'Still, let's push on and try to get under five.'

'It's taken us nearly an hour to do the first four miles.'

'Well, we better get a move on then!'

I found the next two miles particularly tough. We were running along the level gradient of the Slapton Line, but at a pace quicker than my body wanted to go after the stress it had been put through. I then remembered I had swum the length of this bloody road only a few weeks earlier, so

I couldn't really moan about having to run it. I gritted my teeth and kept going.

It was now about 3pm and the sun was out in full force. Out on the bike, the movement of air kept us cool, but on this stretch of coast path, there was no shade and the sandy path reflected the sun back up from below, making you feel like a rotisserie chicken.

By the time we reached Torcross, I felt really nauseous. So much so that I thought I might actually be sick. Stomach issues are something I have generally been very lucky to avoid through all the events I've done. While the rest of my body falls apart, it's very rare for me to experience any stomach or digestive issues (except the incident with the beetroot juice during my Ironman). I decided perhaps I was dehydrated, so forced down some more water. I even cracked open another bag of crisps. Looking back, it might have been the excessive salt from the crisps and the roast potatoes that caused the issues in the first place.

Tim was still talking about the elusive sub-five hour marathon. I didn't want to hold him back, so suggested he go on without me. The steep steps up over the headland from Torcross slowed Tim down to a walk. By the time we reached the seafront at Beesands, I was feeling much better. The feeling of nausea disappeared as quickly as it arrived, demonstrating the remarkable healing power of crisps.

Tim hadn't mentioned our pace for a while and it seemed that he had settled for the fact we might not be as quick as he hoped. I had told him again to run on at his own pace, but he'd kindly stuck with me.

From Beesands, the path climbs steadily for a couple of miles up to the car park at Start Point. In my mind, this section had been very runnable. In practise, it was mostly a walk. Tim and I would encourage each other to run to a particular tree and then allow ourselves a walk before running to another tree.

In order to incorporate the full marathon distance, we had to run down to Start Point lighthouse from the car park and back. This is pretty much the only stretch of tarmac on the entire course, and in my head, this had been a fast, easy section.

As we ran down to the lighthouse, we passed many competitors walking slowly back up the path.

Why were they walking? This is the easy bit. Losers!

As soon as we reached the lighthouse and turned to run back up to the car park, it felt like the gradient had tripled in severity. We ran about 20 metres and then switched to a slow walk back up to the car park.

From Start Point, the path meandered down to the beach and Mattiscombe, and then on past the beaches at Lannacombe and Woodcombe. The coastguard station at Prawle Point - the halfway mark for the course - came into view. It was tantalisingly close but still a couple of miles away and perched at the top of a big hill.

After the turnaround at Prawle Point, we would then retrace our steps all the way back to the finish. This meant that hopefully we would get a chance to see all the other competitors.

Timmy J was by far the quickest of our group and we had seen him coming back the other way, long before the halfway point. He was at least an hour ahead of us. Psychologically, we hoped it would feel easier on the return leg. As we continued onward to Prawle Point, we were still moving further away from where we needed to be.

We reached the halfway point at 6.15pm and were greeted with a well-stocked feed station manned by a local scout group. The entire RMIC had such fantastic marshals and supporters throughout, who had given up their time to help the event go ahead. Hearing encouraging words from a smiling face makes an enormous difference when you are struggling.

We took a few minutes to appreciate the view from this promontory and ate some crisps. I stupidly put another of my roast potatoes into my mouth. It seemed stupid to carry them with me and not eat them, and I didn't have the heart to throw them away. Again, I regretted it instantly but knew I would probably have another.

With an hour to go before sunset, we said our thanks to those manning the feed station and began our return journey.

From mile 15, Tim began feeling really nauseous and couldn't eat or drink anything. He had been setting the pace for most of the first half but was now behind me and very quiet. Strangely, he refused one of my roast potatoes.

We passed John coming the other way. He was about 40 minutes behind us and a spectator friend had joined him for a section of his run. He has also arranged for another friend to meet him at the turnaround point at Prawle Point with a bacon sandwich. I'm glad he had some kind and decent friends, unlike Tim and me.

A mile or so later, we met Claire, Rachel and Kate. Claire had caught them a few miles back and they were all going to run together. It was amazing to see Rachel (and Kate and Claire) and I felt much happier thinking of them running with each other. They were all still smiling and full of enthusiasm. Rachel and I had a quick hug, wished each other luck, and then we continued in opposite directions.

Ross was the next to pass us. He was looking very focused but smiled and we each shouted words of encouragement and gave a fist bump as we passed.

Tim had remained silent for a few miles. He eventually muttered something.

'Sorry, what was that?' I said.

'I said, brilliant, we are back at Mattiscombe.'

I looked again at the beach below us.

'Er... that's not Mattiscombe I'm afraid.'

'Oh, damn. Are we not there yet? We are only at Lannacombe?'

'Er, no, sorry. That's not even Lannacombe. That's Woodcombe. We've got a couple more headlands to get round still.'

Tim's head went down again.

We passed Martin on the rocky section west of Lannacombe. It's a very technical section and Tim and I had not even attempted to run this bit. Martin was on a mission. He gave a proper warrior-style roar and powered past.

'You've got this Martin! Keep going!

I looked at my watch.

'Do you think he'll make it?' I said. 'It's going to be quite tight.'

'I've no idea,' said Tim, still focused on his own suffering. 'I hope so.'

Nine of the eleven were now accounted for. That just left Sophie and Simon. Sophie had been the one to instigate all of this, and the thought of her not making the cutoff was too much to even contemplate.

The sun was very low in the sky now. Sunset was about 30 minutes away, and at that point they would begin closing the feed station at Prawle Point. Any runners who had not made it there in time would have to turn back and not complete the full run.

About 10 minutes after passing Martin, we glimpsed a pair of brightly coloured leggings in the distance and the unmistakable pink hair of Sophie. It was accompanied by a fair amount of whooping from both her and us. Even Tim was brought back from the dead by her energy.

If you bump into Sophie on a run or bike ride, you can get chatting and suddenly an hour will have disappeared. There was no time for that today. Time was running out. Despite being 15 hours into an iron-distance triathlon, and looking likely to miss the cutoff, Sophie was still smiling.

'You've got this, Sophie! You're awesome,' I shouted.

'It's going to be bloody close,' she said. 'But I'll give it my best.'

It was Sophie's pink hair and leggings that came to her advantage in the end. The sun set, twilight fell, and those manning the checkpoint at Prawle Point assumed no more runners would reach the station in time. The sweeper runner would then work his way back along the course, getting runners who had not made it as far as Prawle Point to turn back. They were in the process of packing away the feed station when, through the fading light, they spotted Sophie's pink hair and brightly coloured leggings making their way around the headland. She reached the checkpoint just before it closed and was allowed to begin her return journey.

When we reached the car park at Start Point for the second time, the sun was just beginning to set. Tim's family and friends were there to cheer us on and he sat down on the grass verge and put his head in his hands.

I then spotted Simon standing at the feed station.

'George!' he said jovially. 'How are you doing? Not too far to go now.'

'Hey Si. How are you doing? Have you still got to run to Prawle Point?'

'I didn't make the cutoff for the bike. I missed it by about 15 minutes.'

'Oh, Si. I'm gutted for you. That's really harsh. Can you not just do the full run anyway? You could still get back before midnight.'

'Nah, they've told me because I missed the cut off I can only run to here and back. Just a half marathon for me today. It's a shame, but nevermind.'

'But you're looking so fresh still. I reckon you've still got time to do the full course.'

'It's fine. I've made my peace. I realised halfway through the bike that I wasn't going to make it in time. Today is not my day. There will be another time.'

'I'm really gutted for you, buddy. I love your positive attitude.'

'Well, it's my own fault. I should have swum and cycled a bit quicker. Do you guys need any food? I've got shit loads going spare. I thought I was going to be out running all night.'

'We're fine. Thanks very much.'

'No problem. I'm going to start running back. I'm sure you two will catch me up in no time. Is Tim ok? He doesn't look so great.'

'Yeah, I think he'll be fine. We'll see you in a bit. Well done again.'

We never did catch Simon up. He had the strongest finish of all of us. It was frustrating knowing he would most likely have made it to Prawle Point and back within the cutoff, but it's understandable that the race organisers have to impose cutoffs, especially when trying to limit the time runners spent on the dangerous coast path in the dark.

Tim deteriorated further after leaving Start Point. He was still feeling nauseous and dizzy. His legs had turned to jelly, and he had lost all motivation to continue. We walked across the beach at Hallsands about half an hour after sunset, and the moon was reflecting brightly on the sea. Tim started talking about pulling out of the event for the first time.

'Of course you're not going to pull out,' I said.

'Why not? What's the point of continuing?'

'Because of everything you've done today. And all the training you've put in for the last few months.'

'But it's all pointless really, isn't it? I mean, why are we doing this? We don't even get a medal.'

'If you pull out now, you will be so angry with yourself when you wake up tomorrow.'

'I honestly don't think I will.'

'You definitely will. This will all be over soon. It doesn't matter if we walk the whole way.'

Tim's wife Vienna, and friend Darrell, were there to meet us at Beesands. By this point, the sun had set and it was properly dark. I didn't know if it was irresponsible to keep encouraging Tim to continue when he was feeling so horrendous, but thankfully Vienna and Darrell both tried to get him to keep going, too. Vienna and Darrell walked with us for half a mile, up and over the steep headland between Beesands and Torcross.

It was refreshing to have others to walk with, as I think Tim was probably getting fed up with me.

'Do you think there will be medical help at the finish?' he said.

'What sort of medical help do you need?'

'I don't know. Just something to stop me from feeling like this. I think I need to go on a drip.'

'I don't think you need to go on a drip. You'll be fine.'

'I wish Rory was here,' he said. 'I need Rory. Rory would know what to do.'

Rory was one of the race directors who we had got to know well over the last few months.

'Rory would tell you to stop moaning and keep going.' I said. 'Rory will be there at the finish. It's not long to go now.'

Tim kept telling me to leave him and run on ahead. There was no chance that was going to happen. He had stuck with me earlier in the day when I had been struggling. Now it was my turn. No man left behind.

If I had pushed on, then, yes, I would have been closer to the finish. But at what cost? I would most likely be feeling much worse than I was now. And without Tim there, I would be over-analysing how I was feeling and would have experienced a higher perceived level of suffering. Instead, I had Tim to compare myself to. And compared to him, I was doing bloody brilliantly.

We staggered slowly down the steep steps into Torcross and then had the 2.5 flat miles of the Slapton Line to cover. We met some friends in the car park who had come to cheer us on. Midway through chatting to them, I noticed Tim had staggered off. Thankfully, in the direction we needed to go. He was desperate for it all to be over.

'Right, I better go,' I said. 'Great to see you all. Thanks for coming to cheer us on!'

We had less than five miles to go, and Tim seemed to be improving. The closer we got to the finish, the closer we got to Rory, the more his symptoms seemed to improve.

'Do you mind if I put some music on?' he said.

'Of course not. Is it to drown me out? Am I that annoying?'

'Ha, no, not at all. I just thought it might help take my mind of things.'

He pulled out his phone and I was expecting some motivating power ballad to get us through the final few miles. Instead, he put on some quite obscure progressive house. It was perfect music for the poolside in Ibiza. Stumbling along a sandy footpath in the dark after 16 hours of non-stop exercise, it didn't quite match the vibe. Two minutes later, Tim pulled out his phone again and ended the track.

'Nope, I think that only made it worse.'

The steepest section of the entire run course is situated just over a mile from the finish. The coast path descends deeply into a valley before climbing up the other side. It's a little tricky to navigate as the coast path crosses an open field, and it's not obvious where the main path goes. A network of sheep tracks makes things more confusing. It had been quite challenging to navigate during daylight hours. It's even harder at night.

Fortunately, Rachel and I had run this section just a week before the event, and I knew exactly where we needed to go. The two Marines in front of us, however, did not. They veered off left too soon and were going to descend into the valley via the wrong field. Tim began following behind them.

'Guys, it's this way,' I shouted.

They turned to face me.

'No, George, it's definitely this way,' said Tim, continuing after them.

'I promise you it's not. I did this a week ago. It's this way.'

'I'm sure these guys know what they're doing. I reckon it's this way.'

'GUYS!' I shouted, louder this time. 'YOU'RE GOING THE WRONG WAY!'

'Are you sure, George?'

'100%. That goes down into the wrong part of the valley and there's a barbed wire fence at the bottom.'

All we could see was the glow from their head torches as they continued away from us. Tim was standing halfway between me and them, deciding whether to go with his instinct and follow the Marines, or trust that I knew where I was going.

He paused. Then he turned towards the Marines and shouted after them, telling them they were going the wrong way. By this point, our voices were lost in the wind, and their light faded as they disappeared over the horizon.

They didn't die, by the way. It wasn't a cliff or anything like that. Just the wrong grassy field.

When we watched the trackers a few days later, we found out that Tim's tracker conveniently wasn't transmitting a GPS signal for this section. You can see me right behind these two Marines, just before they disappeared down into the Valley of Death, and then I continue along the correct route and am almost at the finish line by the time they've trudged back up the hill to the proper path.

Still, they are Royal Marines. You would think they should be able to read a map.

Two marshals were stationed at the top of the valley on the other side, and they had the perfect view of people's head torches descending into the valley. They too had apparently shouted to the Marines. They, too, had been ignored.

We could now hear the distant music which we knew must be coming from the race finish, less than a mile away. As we passed through the gate at the top of the last hill before our descent to the finish, Tim and I both gave a gasp. Far down below us, illuminated in the darkness, was the dramatic *finish* arch in the car park at Blackpool Sands.

We then heard cheering and whistling. They could see our head torches at the top of the hill. We returned the cheers, and I gave a feeble whistle, and then we began the final descent.

Tim and I crossed the line together after 16 hours and 19 minutes, and were congratulated immediately by all three race directors. It was an incredible day, with so many feelings and emotions compressed into those 16 hours, 19 minutes. Tim quickly realised it had been right to continue. He would never have forgiven himself for pulling out. He didn't need a drip after all. He didn't even need Rory.

Simon was at the finish, and he was remaining remarkably positive about his experience. He had swum 2.4 miles, cycled 112 miles and ran 13 miles, and still looked sprightly at the end. By anyone's standards, that's a damn impressive achievement.

I could see on the online tracker that Rachel was with Claire and Kate, and they were only about three miles behind. Ross, Martin and Sophie were all still out on the course and still a little way from the finish.

Timmy J had finished a couple of hours before Tim and me and was probably tucked up in bed already.

John finished just five minutes behind us. We had been about 40 minutes ahead at the halfway stage, but while Tim and I had plodded along, John had slowly and steadily caught us up. He also tripped and partially fell off a cliff at one point, and had some impressive grazes on his hands and legs to show for his efforts.

Rachel, Claire and Kate crossed the line together at about 10.50pm. They each had a look of relief, euphoria and disbelief on their faces. I might have shed a tear or two. It turned out they had all been joint first female. A couple of other women didn't start the race, some didn't make the cutoff, and a few were still out on the course. They were awarded a huge framed Royal Marines dagger, which was very cool but completely impractical. They agreed to take it in turns to look after it. Thankfully, Rachel's turn hasn't yet come.

Ross finished strongly about 30 minutes later. We watched a highlights film of the day a couple of weeks later and there was footage of Ross emerging from the sea after his swim. He was the last out of the water, taking 2 hours 40 minutes for his swim. He was in the water for almost an hour longer than me. The thought of that swim being even five minutes longer was unbearable.

The footage was really uncomfortable to watch, and it took Ross a considerable amount of effort to get to his feet and he staggered up the beach like he'd been in a boxing ring for three hours. His first transition took 20 minutes, and it seemed doubtful he would even make it onto his bike. Yet somehow he dug deep and went out and smashed both the bike and the run. It was a truly heroic effort.

The race had a cutoff time of midnight. It was not as strict as official Ironman events where you get marked down as DNF if you're even a second past the cutoff. The brutality of the course for the RMIC requires a bit more flexibility and leniency. But I think most of the competitors would have wanted to get back before midnight, to feel like they had fulfilled the brief, and completed the distance before the clock ticked over into a new day.

We got prior warning for the arrival of each of the remaining finishers when their head torches appeared at the top of the hill and we could shout and cheer, as people had done for Tim and me.

Martin finished at 11.46pm, which considering his staggeringly last-minute turnaround in transition two, was a fantastic achievement. Thankfully, he had decanted the stuff from his cycling jersey at some point during the run, so finished without his rear bollocks bouncing around. To celebrate his achievement, Martin downed a shot of rum as soon as he crossed the finish line. Seconds later, he sprinted (I do not know how he sprinted after the day he'd had) across the car park and threw up in the hedge.

That left just Sophie out on the course.

All this had been Sophie's fault, so it was inconceivable for her not to finish. It was her enthusiasm and positive energy that had convinced the group to believe it was possible. It would be a cruel ending for her to miss out.

A few minutes before midnight, we saw a light at the top of the hill. It was Sophie. We couldn't see the pink hair or bright leggings in the dark, but the familiar whooping (and the GPS tracker) told us it was definitely Sophie.

She crossed the line at 11.57pm, having run the entire way from the halfway turnaround at Prawle Point with the sweeper runner.

It was an almost fairytale finish. From our group of eleven, ten of us completed the full RMIC. There is no doubt that Simon would have got round the full distance if he'd been allowed. His time will come, and when it does, it will feel even more special.

With a field made up of many Marines and ex-Marines, our ragtag bunch of amateurs stood out. But all those involved with the RMIC had been so lovely and welcoming. The race directors had taken us all under their wings and watched us flourish. They all seemed genuinely proud (and I think a little shocked) that we had made it to the finish line with smiles on our faces.

The day after the RMIC, a good friend sent me a message and asked why I hadn't posted about the event on social media.

'I didn't think to,' I replied.

'You're so modest. If it was me, I wouldn't shut up about it for months. I'd be telling everyone.'

'Ha,' I replied. 'Yeah, I am so modest that I will probably just write a book about it instead.'

Writing a book about my events and achievements seems like the ultimate form of bragging; a bit narcissistic. That's honestly not my intention, but perhaps it is a subconscious way for me to have an outlet to share how proud I am. But the RMIC wasn't about me. I was the expert from the group, remember? I was a veteran triathlete compared to Rachel and the other nine. They had been brave (or perhaps naive) enough to sign up to one of the toughest iron-distance triathlons in the world, and had well and truly conquered it. I felt so proud of all of us.

Obviously I was proud of Rachel in particular, who I had watched first-hand develop from a non-runner, to a marathon runner, to a triathlete, to a cyclist, long-distance swimmer, ultra-marathoner, swimrunner, and now an ironman (non-branded).

I couldn't wait to see what she did next.

THIRTEEN

Back in 2019, I entered all of our family into an event called the Muddy Dog Challenge. It's a fund-raising obstacle race, with lots of mud, to raise money for Battersea Dog's Home. And the novelty factor is that you take part with your dog.

The event had been originally scheduled for April 2020. The pandemic then forced it to be moved to October, and then it got shifted another year to October 2021. By this point, Rachel had lost interest in the event (I'm not sure she was ever that interested in the first place, to be honest), the children had all outgrown their t-shirts, Layla didn't want to take part, and the venue moved to somewhere about 1.5 hours from home. It was also the day after we got back from a holiday in Wales.

Leo, Kitty and I were very excited about it, however, so we all agreed to go. Ludo didn't have a clue what was in store, but he seemed pumped by the excitement.

There had been heavy rain for 48 hours before the event, and when we pulled into the makeshift car park, it was already a mud bath. A woman in a high-viz vest directed me towards another marshal. I looked at the sodden grass ahead of me and knew I was unlikely to even make it as far as the parking space.

Sure enough, as I made my way across the car park, the front wheels began spinning. The van has an automatic transmission and seemed intent on doing everything possible to avoid getting any traction.

An absolute unit of a man strode over to try and help, but despite his best efforts, the van was stuck. I was at a diagonal angle in the field, about five metres from the row of cars I was supposed to be parking alongside. Fortunately, the van in front of me had also got stuck in the same place, so I wasn't a complete loser on my own.

'Just leave it there. It will be fine,' said the marshal.

'Are you sure? Sorry about that.'

'It's no problem. You're not the first. I'm sure we can get one of the crew to help tow you out when you're done.'

Layla was adamant she wasn't going to take part, so we said she could wait for us at the finish line. This meant Kitty could wear Leo's t-shirt, and Leo wear Kitty's. Rachel and I got t-shirts too and Ludo also got to wear a special dog bandanna. For the Muddy Dog Challenge, we had to disregard Rachel's rule of not wearing souvenir race t-shirts before completing the race.

The debacle in the car park meant we missed our starting wave, but there was no problem in us joining the next one. I expected an event like this to be full of families like us. There were about 800 people taking part, but almost no children. It turns out few parents choose to drag their kids around a muddy obstacle course in the name of fun. Most of the other competitors were older than us and running solo with their dog.

A fitness instructor went through a proper aerobic warm-up session with us all, involving star jumps, lunges and a series of stretches. Ludo and the other dogs eyed each other up. Some barked. Others growled.

The event took place in the grounds of Escot House in East Devon. Despite being wet underfoot, it was a glorious day and perfect conditions to be taking part. We set off at slightly staggered intervals and the four of us (plus Ludo) made our way across the first field. We let Kitty set the pace, which was nice and relaxed (slow). Ludo was straining at the lead, desperate to get ahead to catch up with the dogs in front.

The first few obstacles were nice and easy. There were tunnels for us to crawl through, ball pits to wade through, and inflatable barriers to climb over. Ludo was having the time of his life. There was no mud involved in the early stages. Most of that was in the car park.

After about 2km, the route split. Runners and muddy dogs had an option to either turn left to complete a longer loop, making up a total of 5km. Or turn right and take the direct route back to the finish totalling 2.5km.

Kitty was ready to call it a day. Rachel hadn't been feeling great on the way to the event, so was more than happy to take the shortcut home with Kitty. Leo and I were keen to do the full loop, and Ludo was loving every minute. So we turned left.

The obstacles got noticeably muddier from here on. We ran through a forest with many deep, mud-filled trenches to wade through (some of them were reminiscent of the car park), and a couple of inflatable pools filled with icy water. One involved dunking your head to get under a barrier. Ludo refused to even get in the water, so a marshal took hold of his lead and walked around it, while Leo and I plunged head first into the pool.

There were a couple of other obstacles where we had to crawl through mud under a cargo net. Again Ludo watched on from the sidelines. He regretted turning left. Leo insisted that we lie on our stomachs for these, rather than crawl through and avoid most of the mud. By the time we finished, we were well and truly coated. Ludo was pretty much spotless. Rachel, Kitty and Layla were there to meet us at the finish line, and we cleaned ourselves off with a hosepipe.

Back in the car park, Ludo got muddier than he had done during the entire event. When our backs were turned, he jumped onto the seats in the back and then the front of the van, using the upholstery as a makeshift towel. Rachel lost her shit completely. I found it hard not to laugh.

A member of staff in a 4-wheel-drive was on hand to come and tow us out and we made it out of the car park without further incident. Forget triathlons, swimruns or ultramarathons, running 5km with your family and your dog is much more my kind of event.

FOURTEEN

For my birthday present earlier in the year, Rachel entered us both into a running event called the Lone Wolf. The Lone Wolf is a backyard ultra that takes place in the Dartington Estate in South Devon. A backyard ultra is a race format devised by Gary Cantrell, the legend behind *The Barkley Marathons* (watch the Netflix documentary if you haven't already seen it - it's brilliant). Competitors have to run a lap of 4.167 miles within an hour. Then every hour, on the hour, they begin a new lap. The race continues until there is one person remaining. One lone wolf.

The reason for the obscure 4.167 mile distance (or 6706 metres), is that if you can keep going and run a lap every hour for 24 hours, you will cover exactly 100 miles.

4.167 miles sounds like nothing. You could even walk it at a very brisk pace.

But that's the beauty of the format. It is so easy to start with but quickly becomes very difficult. If you're not ready at the start line on the hour, you're out. And you can choose to quit at any point.

I was reluctant to do The Lone Wolf as it was only three weeks after the RMIC. I also felt a bit like we were dumping our children regularly while we went off selfishly taking part in these events. I mentioned this to the kids, and it turned out they were desperate for us to dump them. They preferred their weekends staying at friends' houses to weekends with us.

The Lone Wolf was self-supported, which meant we had to bring all our own food. Sorting nutrition for a backyard ultra is quite a challenge. Partly because we could potentially (although unrealistically) be running up to 100 miles. Also, we had no idea what sort of foods we would want to eat, or be able to stomach after being on our feet for such a long time.

From previous experience at the East Devon Round, I knew that real food seemed to be the best. So we packed everything: ham sandwiches, cheese sandwiches, crisps, Spanish tortilla, apples, bananas, brownies, flapjack, sweets. Rachel is incapable of estimating quantities and always vastly over prepares. She baked a double batch of flapjacks and a double batch of brownies, and packed them all to take with us.

We loaded all our snacks into the two big plastic boxes we had used during the RMIC transition. We left these enormous boxes directly next to the Lone Wolf start line. Several of the other competitors took the piss out of the ridiculous amount of food we had brought.

The race began at a respectable time of 10am, which was very refreshing compared to the usual pre-dawn start of most endurance events. Depending on how long we lasted, it could be a very antisocial finishing time with the race potentially lasting the distance until 10am the following morning.

From an organisational point of view, a backyard ultra looks like a dream. The entire thing seemed to be put on by two men. It was all off-road, so there were no marshals or road closures to worry about, and we all signed a waiver beforehand, which presumably released them of any liability (I obviously didn't read it).

It was an eclectic mix of people gathered on the start line for the Lone Wolf, ranging in age from 18 to about 70. It was a relatively small field, with 40 runners taking part. The organisers talked us through the rules and then there was a countdown from 10, and when we reached zero, we all had to howl like a wolf as we began each lap.

One of the organisers guided us around the first lap to familiarise all the runners with the route. It was a tougher, more technical course than I was expecting. We wound our way through the beautiful woodland of the Dartington Estate. There were many tree roots to navigate, branches to dodge, and rocks to avoid. Thankfully, there had been no recent rain, and it was not too muddy underfoot. We emerged from the woods after about 2.5 miles and then the final 1.5 miles followed a meadow alongside the River Dart before climbing up a gravel lane back to the start. The first lap took us 45 minutes. Regardless of how long the lap took, we could not start the second lap until the beginning of the next hour.

After the first 4.167 miles of running, neither Rachel nor I were ready to make a start on our treasure trove of goodies yet. We had a quick swig of water and then spent the leftover 15 minutes chatting to the other runners. Some sat down on the sofas in the little hut by the start line, others made a hot drink in the kitchen, but all those who began lap 1 were at the start line ready for lap 2.

After another countdown and another howl (we were already in the swing of things), we began our second lap. It felt very different to the first and the field spread out quickly as people ran at their own pace, rather than at the pace set by the race organiser. The start of the loop went up a track for about 100 metres and most of us chose to walk this steep bit. Some of the speedy runners powered away like they were in a sprint.

We got chatting to a woman named Hannah on lap 2. Hannah had done a similar array of events to Rachel and me. She had taken part in a handful of long-distance runs, but this was her first ever backyard ultra. Like Rachel and me, she wasn't particularly fast either. But Hannah's determination and drive were in a different league.

'Do you have a target in mind of how far you want to run?' asked Rachel.

'I'm here to win it,' said Hannah confidently.

'Oh wow, that's cool.'

'Yeah. When I put my mind to something, I tend to achieve it.'

It was at this point I knew I certainly wouldn't be leaving this event as the last man standing - the Lone Wolf.

The second lap took us 48 minutes, which included a few short walks up the steeper hills, and then steady running for the rest of the loop.

A couple of runners reached the end of lap 2 and called it a day. They received a big round of applause and congratulations from the rest of us. 8.4 miles of trail running is still a very respectable distance. And it was the furthest either had ever run.

I was already a big fan of the backyard ultra race format. When taking part in usual running events, the starting gun sounds and from then on, you only see people who have covered the distance at the same speed as you. On some events, with a smaller number of entrants, the field can spread out so quickly that you are soon on your own and you might not see another competitor all the way to the finish.

The beauty of the backyard ultra format is that regardless of how fast you are, when the next hour begins, you are back on that start line with everyone else.

Some speedy runners completed the loop in under 40 minutes and then had 20 minutes to rest and recover. Some even lay down for a quick nap, or cooked a quick meal between laps. Others timed their run so that they arrived back at the start with seconds to spare until the next one. Most of our laps took between 48 and 50 minutes.

And on each lap we got chatting to different people.

We met Ryan. Ryan had driven down from Bristol on his own to take part. He had never run over 10 miles before, so lap 3 was taking him into unknown territory. He had booked an AirBnb nearby for the weekend, but it turned out it was basically someone's tiny shed with a bed in it, and he had got very little sleep the night before the race.

We met Josiah. Josiah was only 18 and not only was the Lone Wolf his first ever backyard ultra, it was his first ever running event. While other runners slowly build up, maybe starting with parkrun, 10k, and then a half marathon. Josiah had entered a race that might be 100 miles and 24 hours long.

But that is the appeal of the format. He knew he could get round one lap, and then he would see what he was capable of. Josiah had struggled with his mental health through his teenage years. He began running as a means to address this, and it had turned his life around. None of his school friends were into running, so he entered the Lone Wolf as a chance to meet and run with like-minded people. The furthest he had ever run was 13 miles the week before the Lone Wolf while on holiday in Scotland with his parents.

At the end of lap 4, there was no sign of Ryan, the guy from Bristol who was sleeping in the shed. As the countdown began for lap 5, we saw him approach. But as we all howled to begin the lap, he was still just short of the line, which meant his race was over. He had apparently started walking midway through the lap and then just miscalculated how long he had to get back to the finish.

At the end of lap 5, Ryan was still there watching. He seemed disappointed and annoyed with himself. Four laps was still further than he had ever run before, but he had hoped to experience running in the dark. It was 2pm, and sunset was not until closer to 7pm. But he also couldn't face heading back to his shed for the night, so decided to stick around and watch the race, and then once the sun set, he would pull on his head torch and join us for a few night laps.

Despite being early October, it was very mild. John, a runner who had travelled all the way from the Midlands, had his shirt off on lap 2 and it stayed off for the rest of the day. The furthest he had ever previously run was 10 miles. Less than three laps. He made it back to the start just before lap 4 with a minute to spare. He stopped because it was already the furthest he had ever gone.

'Why don't you start this lap and see how you get on?' we suggested. 'It doesn't matter if you finish it?'

'Oh god,' he said. 'I suppose I could.'

He grabbed a quick swig of drink and then was ready to begin lap 5. The exact same thing happened at the end of lap 5. He had brought very little food with him, having only planned to do three or four laps. Fortunately, we had enough to feed everyone, so he agreed to try one more lap to see what happened.

We met Andy. Andy won the inaugural Lone Wolf two years previously. He then came back to defend his title the following year, but was beaten by a couple of Royal Marines (they get everywhere) who seemingly would have kept running for days. Andy explained how psychological tactics played an important part in a race like this. Rather than convincing others to run one more lap, like Rachel and I were doing, you should be encouraging others to quit. He said how the first year he had asked people whether they were going to be ok going into work tired the next day, only for them to pull out at the end of the next lap. When hearing that another runner had left their dog with a neighbour for the first time, he asked on a later lap if they had heard anything from the neighbour and whether they were sure the dog was ok. That runner pulled out at the end of the lap, too.

Andy had made it clear he was in it until the bitter end, too. But unlike Hannah, rather than just wanting to be the last man standing, Andy had set out to run 100 miles, regardless. Even if others all dropped out by halfway, Andy was going to keep going for the full 24 hours.

If Hannah's confidence hadn't sealed the deal for me quitting, then Andy's bravado almost did. But I was never there to win it. I had no intention of running 100 miles. I didn't want to run for 24 hours. Leo had a football match at 10am the following morning and I had semi-promised I would be there for that. And I was hoping to have some sleep between then and now.

Shirtless John was looking more and more tired, but he kept agreeing to do one more lap. And he kept getting back to the finish just in time, so kept beginning more and more. He eventually called it a day after 8 laps. That's over 33 miles. Having previously never run further than 10. It was incredible to witness the stories and determination of fellow runners during the day.

There were other experienced runners, who at the start of lap 1 looked like the ultimate athletes. They dashed off at quite a pace and always had loads of time to spare at the end of each lap. Most of these had called it a day before John.

We were down to about 10 runners. 18-year-old Josiah was still going strong. He too spent each lap making all sorts of strange agonising noises, declaring it was definitely his last lap. Josiah had planned to do four laps - over 16 miles - and his longest ever run. He had arranged for his mum to come and collect him at 2pm. She was waiting for him at the end of lap 4, and he told her he was going to aim for another two. She lived nearby, so agreed to come back two hours later.

Apart from one lap when Josiah sprinted off, setting the day's fastest recorded lap in the process (39 minutes), Rachel and I ran almost all of his laps with him. He was enormously entertaining and very inspiring. I tried to remember what I would have been doing aged 18. Running multiple laps of a wood with a bunch of strangers would have been at the bottom of my list of desirable ways to pass the time.

After six laps, Josiah was feeling better than he had done after four (probably because of the cocktail of painkillers he had been taking). He had no intention of stopping yet. His mum was there at 4pm, as requested, but agreed to come back at 6pm to collect Josiah after lap 8 - almost 34 miles. I already had a feeling he would not be stopping then.

There were now about eight of us left. If you had taken a guess at the start line, we would have been the least likely eight to come out on top. All the other fitter, leaner, sportier, more athletic runners had called it a day. It was a proper case of the hare and the tortoise.

During lap 8, Josiah stubbed his toe on a rock.

'Ahh, fucking shit,' he muttered. 'Oh, sorry, I didn't mean to swear.'

'Ha!' I laughed, slightly shocked not by his swearing but by his apology.

'I'm still a bit unsure about swearing around old people,' he said.

I looked around, assuming we must have just passed some elderly walkers. And then I realised he was talking about Rachel and me. I burst out laughing again.

'Sorry, I didn't mean you are old, I just... I just... I just... you know...'

Initially, I felt a little offended. Rachel and I regularly get teased and called old by our own children, but I think this was the first time that either of us had ever been described as old by someone not related.

But I can remember when I was a teenager, chatting to friends of my parents who would probably have been in their early 40s, like we were now, and considering them old.

'It's fine. You're right. We are about 24 years older than you, so I suppose that makes us old. Swear as much as you fucking like.'

From then on, I like to think Josiah saw me as a really cool old person.

Josiah's mum returned at the end of lap 8 - 6pm. This time, he was undecided about whether to carry on. Part of me wanted to encourage him to keep going. The other part thought it was a bit irresponsible to try to persuade an 18-year-old who had just run over 33 miles in his first ever event to keep going.

'What about two more laps?' I said. 'That will take you over 40 miles.'

Josiah sighed. 'Oh, go on then.'

His mum rolled her eyes, but there was a glint in them accompanied by a smile that showed she was in awe of what her son was doing. 'I'll be back in a couple of hours,' she said. 'Take care.'

Having been watching from the sidelines since 2pm and waiting for darkness, Ryan joined us for the 6pm lap, just as the sun was setting. There was no need for head torches just yet, but he decided it could act as his warm up before the proper darkness set in on the 7pm lap.

In his mind, 4.16 miles hadn't sounded too bad. In reality, with the tree roots and the terrain, he had forgotten how hard going it was. But he'd had a nice four hour break, so should be raring to go.

'How did you find that?' I said at the end of lap 9. 'Looking forward to running in the dark?'

'Nah, fuck that. I'm done. It was much more fun watching from the sidelines. I'm going to watch a few more laps and then head back to my shed.'

The more tired our legs became, the more precarious the tree roots appeared. As early as lap 3, we were behind a man who caught his foot and fell hard on the floor. We helped him up and checked he was ok, and that he was able to continue running. I almost fell a few times in the late afternoon. In the early evening, Rachel caught her toe on a tree root and came very close to face-planting into the trunk of another tree.

On lap 9, just as it was getting dark, she somehow tripped while we ran along the flat grassy meadow section of the run. It wasn't just a small stumble. It was a full-on front flip. She somersaulted the entire way, head over heels, and landed hard on her hip.

'Oh shit, are you ok? That looked nasty.'

'Yes, I think so,' she said. 'My side hurts quite a lot.'

Rachel hobbled her way through the remaining two miles of lap 9 and said she would see how it felt before deciding whether to continue. We made it back to the start, stretched, ate, and switched on our head torches.

'So, are we going to start lap 10?' I said.

'I'll give it a go and see how I get on. I think this might be my last lap, though. My hip is really sore.'

'Ok, well, we'll try to get round this lap.'

'How am I going to cope in the dark when I wiped out totally on a flat bit when it was still light?'

'I'm not sure. It was pretty spectacular. Let's just take it nice and easy. We can go a bit slower in the dark and still get round in under an hour.'

My goal had always been to try to get to 12 laps. 50 miles. That sounded like a very respectable distance. And we would be home in time for *Match of the Day*. But after about the fourth lap, I thought getting to 12 was perhaps unrealistic.

Lap 10 felt like the longest of the day by far. Probably because it was our slowest lap. Despite running the same 4 mile loop since 10am that morning, we still didn't feel completely familiar with the route. Especially in the dark. It wasn't until another runner - who had been paying more attention than us - pointed out that we were going the wrong way, and we realised a couple of the arrows had been switched around by meddling walkers (or perhaps sneaky fellow competitors). Thankfully, we were soon back on track.

Early in lap 10, Rachel decided she was calling it quits at the end of the lap. Running was causing too much discomfort since her fall. I had no intention of continuing without her. Despite our competitiveness, I would have got no satisfaction at doing an extra lap just to beat her by one. Instead, I got ridiculously excited about gaining an extra two hours on the 10pm finish I had initially expected. We could maybe pick up a takeaway and watch a film and still be done in time for *Match of the Day*. It was the happiest I had felt all day.

'You should do another couple of laps,' said Rachel. 'At least get to 12 laps. That's 50 miles. You had that as your goal.'

'Yeah, but now my goal is to get home two hours earlier.'

'I think you should do another two. I honestly don't mind waiting.'

'I honestly don't want to.'

Josiah, who had been running with us all lap but had been very quiet, suddenly spoke up.

'I'll run another two with you, George,' he said.

'You want to do more? This is your first ever running event and you want to run 50 miles?'

'Yeah, why not? I can no longer feel my body anyway.'

Josiah seemed to have somehow transcended all the pain he had been experiencing since early in the afternoon.

'Nah, I think I'm going to quit while I'm ahead,' I said. 'I'm happy to call it a day at 10.'

We made it back to base with ten minutes to spare, and I went to tell the organiser we were tapping out.

'Just wait five minutes before we decide,' said Rachel.

I knew this meant she wasn't done.

'Maybe we should do one more lap?' she said a couple of minutes later.

'It's up to you. You said you could barely move a few minutes ago.'

'Let's give it a go. One more lap.'

'Ok, fine. One more lap.'

We went to tell Josiah we were going to head out for lap 11, but he had taken the decision (partly due to pressure from his mum, who had been growing increasingly concerned about her son) to end his race. An 18-year-old taking part in his first ever running race and completing 42 miles was just incredible. He was such an inspiring person and Rachel and I felt very honoured to have had a chance to run many of those 42 miles with him.

It was also quite satisfying to prove that we two old people could just about outrun him.

I had genuinely been delighted to be finishing after 10, but it now looked hopeful we would get to 12. About seven of us remained. Hannah, the woman we met on lap 2 who was out to win it, looked as sprightly as she had at the beginning. There was still a steely determination in her eyes. There was also another woman, Kirsten, who had said very little during the day. She had a keen group of supporters at the end of each lap, and she seemed to be planning to go the distance.

Running in the dark with a head torch ended up being much easier than we expected. Something about the beam of light illuminating a relatively small patch of pathway ahead meant we had to focus even more carefully on our footing. Running in daylight, our eyes were free to wander to the passing trees, the river running alongside the meadow, the walkers and picnickers, and our fellow runners. When navigating through the woods in the dark, however, your focus is dialled right in to the narrow bit of ground illuminated by the head torch. Your concentration becomes laser-focused and extra care is taken on your footing.

Rachel was still in a lot of discomfort but had decided to finish lap 11. Then if lap 12 was to be our last lap, we didn't have to make it back by the end of the hour, so could take our time a little.

At the end of lap 11, as we approached the finish, I heard a familiar voice up ahead in the darkness. It was Simon. He had called in to see how we were getting on. It is amazing what a mental and physical boost you can get from seeing a friend when you are feeling so low. We only had time for a very brief chat before it was time to howl at the start of our final lap, but the fact he had gone out of his way to come and cheer us on was really touching.

Six of us began lap 12. Andy, Hannah, Kirsten, Oliver, Rachel and me. We hadn't chatted much to Oliver as he had always been quicker than us. Despite her determination, Kirsten was having knee problems and didn't think she could go for much longer. Hannah was still claiming to plan to go the distance, but the steely determination had faded a bit from her eyes. Andy was looking annoyingly energetic and was continuing to practise his mind games. He was still talking about running all 24 laps, regardless of whoever was left.

We ran with Andy on lap 12. He was trying to encourage us to keep going. He knew we weren't threats to becoming the Lone Wolf, and I think he wanted some company for a few more laps. Especially as there would be another six or seven laps to go before it began to get light again. It was going to be a long old night for him.

'When you're driving home, won't you regret not doing one more?' he said.

I thought about it for a moment.

'No, I honestly don't think I will. I came with the aim of maybe doing 12 laps. I've got no desire to run all night, so I'm very happy to call it a day.'

'What about you, Rachel?' he said.

'I should have called it a day a few laps ago. I definitely won't be running any further.'

We were slowing considerably. Rachel's hip was troubling her, and she had a couple of big blisters that were also causing a lot of pain. At this pace, there was a good chance we might not be back in time by the end of the hour. This didn't matter to us, but Andy realised that it was looking tight for him, so skipped off ahead. We walked a bit and decided it didn't matter how long it took us to finish.

With a mile to go, we realised we should at least try to get to the start line to cheer the others off, as they had done for us. So we dug deep and covered the final mile, reaching the finish line at about 9.59pm, a minute under 12 hours since we first lined up at the start.

I told Rachel I was going to tell the organiser we were quitting, and this time, she didn't try to stop me. Oliver also called it a day at 12.

That meant just three runners remained - Hannah, Kirsten, and Andy. So Rachel, Oliver and I finished joint 4th (if that's a thing), out of a field of 40. We were delighted with that.

We howled as Andy, Hannah and Kirsten began lap 13, wished them all luck and began the slow trudge back to our van.

I messaged Andy the following morning to find out what happened after we left. Kirsten dropped out a lap after us. Hannah managed another one and a half before calling it a day, and then Andy ran a solo victory lap to finish on 15. Once everyone had packed up and gone home and he had been crowned the Lone Wolf, he decided that running laps through a dark wood on your own for another seven hours was not too appealing. So he called it a day too. And who could blame him?

In May 2022, at a backyard ultra event in Rettert in Germany, Belgian Merijn Geerts set the current record for a distance covered in a backyard ultra. He completed 90 laps, 90 hours (that's nearly four days and four nights) covering a staggering 375 miles. Keith Russell from Ireland completed a lousy 89 laps (371 miles) and would have been marked down as DNF.

I thoroughly enjoyed the format of the backyard ultra and think that it's going to become incredibly popular. It's definitely the most sociable type of running event out there, where a mixed bunch of varying ability of runners can become friends over the course of a few hours, all by appearing on that same start line on the hour, every hour.

I thought about what Andy had said on our last lap. Would I not regret doing one more lap? As we headed home, I had no regrets whatsoever. Yes, I probably could have managed a few more laps. That doesn't mean I wish I had. What would that have achieved? I would just be arriving home later and more tired. I had no desire to go all night. I did not want it enough.

I was there for Leo's football match the next day. A little tired and achy after 12 hours of running. But at least I could sit on the grass in the sun for an hour or so watching the game. Some people claim they push themselves in endurance events to make their kids proud. I'm certain Leo would have preferred me to be at his football match than still running through a wood in pursuit of victory.

As I hobbled towards the pitch, Leo's coach approached me with a flag in his hand.

'Are you happy to be linesman today, George?'

My heart sank.

'Er... yeah, sure. No problem.'

FIFTEEN

In November, a group of nine of us took part in the Exeter Marathon - my third time running this event. Simon was trying again for his first sub four-hour marathon. Twice he had asked me to pace him. Twice he had just missed out. This time I didn't get the call.

It's an extremely flat course and I set off with the hope of getting a PB. Things went well for the first 18 miles and then my willpower evaporated. Ross caught me up and we ran the last few miles together, crossing the line in 3h 48m, which I think was my third fastest ever, and an incredible PB for Ross by about 25 minutes.

Rachel had been suffering with a heavy cold and sinusitis and only made the decision to run on the morning of the race. It was a two-loop course, and when she reached the end of the first loop, she decided to call it a day. One of the race marshals saw her sitting on the wall and somehow talked her into continuing. Midway through the second half, Rachel met up with her close fried Caz who was taking part in her first official marathon (having completed two of her own DIY marathons during the pandemic), and the two of them finished the race smiling together.

It was a nervy wait for Simon. With his disappointment at not finishing the full RMIC, I couldn't bear the thought of him not achieving this goal too.

With three minutes to go before the elusive four-hour mark, Simon came into view. There were plenty of tears, not just from him this time, but from all of us on the sidelines cheering him on. He crossed the line with two and a half minutes to spare. After two failed attempts at a sub four-hour marathon with me as his pacer, he fared much better on his own. It turns out I was the problem.

Everything is slow to arrive in Devon.

When growing up in Northampton, we used to joke that if we missed a film at the cinema, we could just watch it while on holiday in Devon six months later. It can take a little while for news, ideas and trends to filter down to us on our little peninsula.

This also applied to Covid.

During the first and second waves, areas of Devon occupied several of the top ten spots for the lowest rates of Covid in the UK. We only ever heard of friends of friends of friends contracting it, and there were very few local cases.

Even during the summer of 2020, when staycations were all the rage, people flocked to Devon and Cornwall in their thousands, and the health services braced for a major surge in infections. It never came, and the tourists returned home and took their Covid with them.

It wasn't until October 2021 - over 18 months after the start of the pandemic - that Covid finally took hold in South Devon. As case numbers fell in all other parts of the country, Covid rates skyrocketed in Devon. Each day, we got emails from the children's schools about more reported cases.

One evening, I picked Layla and five of her friends up from the cinema and dropped them home. The next day, three of those friends tested positive. Somehow, Layla and I dodged it. It spread through the secondary school rapidly and most of Layla's year group got it in the space of a few weeks. Then Leo's class became infected.

Then it hit the primary school.There are 30 children in Kitty's class at school. At one point, 17 of them were off with Covid. Thankfully, by this point, it was a weaker strain and nobody seemed to get too ill.

Despite the rapidly rising cases, there were no restrictions in place at this point (except for those who tested positive), so life carried on as normal for us. Albeit in a slightly *28 Days Later* meets *Final Destination* sort of way. It was only a matter of time.

I drove Leo to his weekly football training session one Thursday evening in late November, and just as I pulled into the road where his pitch was, the van's engine died. I turned it off and on again. The lights all flashed. There was an ominous clicking, but no sign of life. We were blocking all access to the car park, but thankfully, a group of teenage school kids saw me looking flustered and helped push the van to the side of the road.

I phoned the breakdown recovery who told me it might be a couple of hours, so Leo and I went to his football training. Midway through the session, I got a call to say they had arrived, so we gave our apologies to the coach and rushed back to the van.

The breakdown guy thought it seemed like an issue with the alternator. It was not something he could fix at the roadside, so he offered to tow us home because all local garages were closed for the day.

With no vehicle for the school run the next day, Layla and Leo had to set off extra early to walk the two hilly miles to school. Kitty still had another half an hour until she needed to leave, and as she often did when she was bored, she did a Covid test. Despite having no symptoms, it came up positive.

'Get in!' she shouted. 'No school for at least a week!'

'What do we do about Layla and Leo?' said Rachel. 'What happens if they are positive and we've just sent them into school?'

'I'll phone them and get them to go and have a test done at school. They won't have got there yet.'

15 minutes later, Layla sent a photo of her negative test with the message, *I ain't got Covid bros.* Leo sent a photo of a Covid test, and he had drawn a second red line on his phone app with the caption, *Can I come home?*

Ha, nice try, but no.

Later that evening, Leo tested positive, too.

Kitty still had no symptoms. Leo was feeling a little off, but not too bad.

I phoned various mechanics in town and they were all either fully booked, on holiday, or off with Covid. The only place I could find was about ten miles away and they might not be able to look at it for another week. But they could come and tow it from our house. Layla had been enjoying walking to and from school recently, so it felt serendipitous that our van broke down on the same day that we no longer relied on it for the school run.

After 20 months of being cautious, keeping our distance, being careful of what we touched and avoiding contact with other people, there were now two cases in the house. There was a strange sense of inevitability and acceptance that we would all get it. For me, the fear factor of Covid vanished instantly and it felt like a relief to know I would soon have it.

It didn't seem fair to shut Leo and Kitty away in their rooms for ten days, so they didn't isolate fully from us. We avoided hugs and kisses and I didn't eat their leftover dinner (this was the hardest bit for me). But I knew Covid was coming for us all.

Much to her annoyance, Layla was still required to go to school as normal. If she didn't, it would be marked down as an unauthorised absence. She did a Covid test each morning before school.

We all sat watching TV in the same room in the evening, Leo and Kitty on a separate sofa, and Layla sat at the far end of the lounge with her face mask on. When her close friends had Covid, Layla had not been worried about whether she got it. Catching Covid from one of her friends was acceptable. But for some reason, when her siblings had it, that was much worse. To Layla, Leo and Kitty had Dirty Covid and there was no way she wanted to catch that. If she was going to get Covid, it would be from one of her friends. Not her annoying brother and sister.

At about midnight, we heard Leo shouting from his room. Rachel elbowed me and rolled over and went back to sleep. It was her subtle way of letting me know it was my duty to go and check on him.

When I entered Leo's room, I found him sitting up in bed, very upset and agitated. He kept asking if I was going to stop them from coming through the walls.

'Stop who coming through the walls, pal?' I asked.

'They are trying to get through the walls. Please stop them,' he said, anxiously looking over his shoulder.

His temperature was ridiculously high, his forehead was beaded in sweat, and he was very confused. I gave him some Calpol and sat with him for 20 minutes as his hallucinations slowly began to fade.

He continued to be very upset and I put my arm around him and told him it was all going to be ok. He then started coughing and spluttering loudly. I knew there was no way I would dodge Covid this time. Leo has a downstairs bedroom, so I dragged a mattress into the lounge and slept next to his bedroom in case he needed me in the night.

He was feeling a lot better by morning, and he and Kitty spent the day watching *Harry Potter* movies while Layla begrudgingly went off to school. I was fairly sure I would soon have Covid, so cancelled my few commitments for the week. Leo's hallucinations happened the following night, too. I slept in the lounge again.

The following morning, I walked Ludo with Layla half the way to her school. As we walked up the big hill near our house, I felt a little out of breath. It's a hill I always pant my way up if running or cycling, but it's never felt much effort when walking. As soon as I got home, I did another test. This time, two lines showed up.

I went into the lounge to show my positive lateral flow to Rachel. By the time I returned to the kitchen, I had *get well soon* messages from Rachel's mum, sister, and one of her friends.

'You didn't waste any time telling people,' I called to Rachel.

'I thought I should let people know.'

I think perhaps Rachel's competitive nature was kicking in, too. Me getting Covid before her was a minor victory for Rachel. It proved she had the better immune system than me. Although I'm not sure hers could have withstood 20 minutes of Leo's coughing and spluttering.

When Layla got home from school later that day, she seemed mightily disappointed with me. When Leo and Kitty had been the Covid patients, it had been them and us. The ill and the sick. Now I was one of *them*. She looked at me with contempt, like I had let her down.

Self-isolation rules were still in place when I got Covid in early December 2021 and I didn't leave the house for ten days. Not even to check the postbox. I could have taken Ludo out for walks in the fields where we live, but I felt a bit like I would be taking advantage. Ludo was getting more exercise than normal with Rachel keen to spend as much time as possible out of the Covid house.

Rachel certainly made the most of her freedom. The day after I tested positive, she went out and ran her December marathon. She wanted to get it in just in case she came down with it, too. The second day, she went out for a walk all day. The third, she walked the ten miles to the garage to collect the van.

I stayed at home with Leo and Kitty and watched the eight *Harry Potter* movies on a loop.

I spent five nights in total on a mattress in the lounge. Partly because Leo was still having hallucinations at night. But also to try and keep Rachel away from Covid for a little longer.

I felt fine for the first couple of days. Then developed a slight sinus pain and lost my sense of taste and smell. Rachel made a vegetable curry and I rudely asked her if she had forgotten to put any flavour in it.

Our biggest concern was buying a Christmas tree. Getting the Christmas tree has always been my duty. I used to find it quite stressful but grew to enjoy the process of selecting a tree and bringing it home.

We were concerned that Rachel would test positive too and then we would be treeless. While she was still Covid-free, she went out with Layla one evening to buy one.

Our house is a barn conversion, and the lounge has a double-height ceiling. Each year, we think it might be our last renting this house, so buy a bigger tree to make the most of the extra space. Then another year goes by and it's Christmas again. So we buy an even bigger tree. The one I had bought the previous year was a ten-footer and the fairy was squashed against the rafters, so we had pretty much reached our limit.

While Rachel was out, I had a series of panicked text messages from her stressing about whether she had found a good one or not. And then Layla sent a series of selfies looking genuinely scared. To be fair, it was dark, windy and rainy, which can't be the most enjoyable conditions to choose a tree.

Layla looked pretty traumatised when she got back.

'Please can you choose the tree again next year,' said Layla. 'That was not fun at all.'

Despite the rage, Rachel had picked an absolute belter. I think it was the best tree we have ever had.

I made a speedy recovery from Covid and managed to squeeze in my December Marathon just before Christmas. I ran with Tim and we spent five hours reminiscing about the RMIC. It turns out he would have regretted it if he had pulled out with five miles to go. Who'd have thought?

Layla and Rachel stayed Covid free (for 2021, at least) and the in-laws all came to stay for a fantastic big family Christmas. We managed sea dips on Christmas Eve, Christmas Day and Boxing Day, and we saw out the year with another on New Year's Eve.

2020 had been the year when things did not happen. We made up for it in 2021. As years go, it was certainly one of our most eventful. It began with two months of homeschooling and ended with three of the five of us getting Covid. In between, I published a series of six books, and had researched and written a decent chunk of another.

2021 was a year of firsts. Our first 100k run. My first broken bone. Our first swimrun event, and our first ever backyard ultra. Rachel did her first iron-distance triathlon, and we did our first event with Ludo.

It had been a year of learning, too. I learned about the peppered moth, and I learned about dramatic mixed-media artwork. I learned that broken bones heal. I learned it is possible to over-salt your roast potatoes. I learned the importance of seeing friends and family (and complete strangers) during your time of need. I learned no man should be left behind.

I learned that we need to believe.

I learned that I don't have the desire (or ability) to push myself faster or further than others. And that's ok. Because I also learned that getting to the finish line is good enough for me, however long it takes.

Author's note

Thank you for choosing to read my book. If you enjoyed it, I would be extremely grateful if you would consider posting a short review on Amazon and help spread the word about my books in any way you can.

Book Eight?

The *Did Not Finish* books are an ongoing series. To be notified when Book Eight is released, please sign up to my mailing list here

www.georgemahood.com/contactgeorge

or keep an eye on my social media channels.

www.facebook.com/georgemahood
www.instagram.com/georgemahood
www.twitter.com/georgemahood

Signed copies of all of my books are available in my website's 'shop'.

In the meantime, if you haven't already, please check out my other books.

Also by George Mahood

Free Country: A Penniless Adventure the Length of Britain

Every Day Is a Holiday

Life's a Beach

Operation Ironman: One Man's Four Month Journey from Hospital Bed to Ironman Triathlon

Not Tonight, Josephine: A Road Trip Through Small-Town America

Travels with Rachel: In Search of South America

How Not to Get Married: A no-nonsense guide to weddings… from a photographer who has seen it ALL

(available in paperback, Kindle and audiobook)

Acknowledgments

First thanks go to all the organisers, marshals and volunteers for putting on these races. Many of them stand outside all day in horrendous conditions, often with no reward or incentive other than the satisfaction of being a part of the event. And perhaps the joy of watching us suffer.

Special thanks to our family and friends who regularly step in to help with childcare while Rachel and I are taking part in these events.

Rachel's editing job for these books was not as scrupulous as usual, which she claimed was because she enjoyed them so much. I think that is only because she features so prominently in them. She would often write 'LOL' in the margin, even though she had been sitting next to me while reading and hadn't made a murmur. Anyway, thank you for lolling (internally).

Becky Beer was as ruthless as ever with the red pen during her proofreading. That's a compliment. Thank you! Please check out her Bookaholic Bex blog (www.bookaholicbex.wordpress.com) and Facebook page.

Thanks to Robin Hommel and Miriam for additional proofreading and feedback.

Thanks to all our friends who have taken part in these challenges and adventures with us. It is always reassuring to not be the only ones with a ridiculously stupid concept of 'fun'.

Thanks to Rachel... AGAIN (she's even got a starring role in the acknowledgements) for reluctantly agreeing to take part in many of these events with me. We are not always perfect running. cycling, swimming partners, but I wouldn't want it any other way.

Thanks to Layla, Leo and Kitty for putting up with your annoying parents and for continuing to inspire and amuse us. Hopefully one day you will look back and be glad we dragged you out on all these walks.

Thanks to my mum and dad for dragging me out on all those walks when I was younger. I didn't appreciate it at the time, but I do now.

Lastly, thanks to you for reading this series. The idea that people enjoy reading about random things I get up to still feels very bizarre to me, but I'm always honoured and grateful.

Big love.

Made in the USA
Middletown, DE
15 August 2022

71343338R00109